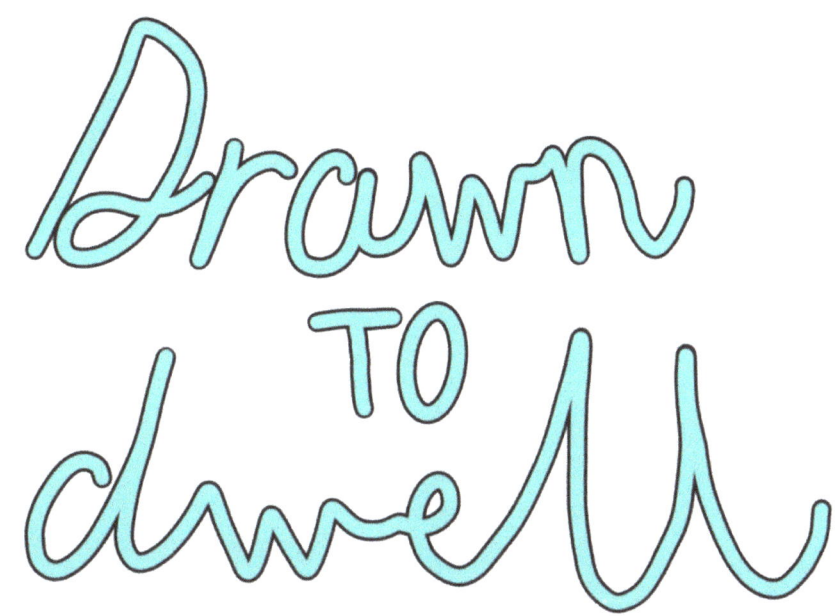

ADULT COLOURING
Rebecca Johnston

Copyright © 2024 Rebecca Johnston.

All rights reserved. No part of this book may be used or reproduced by any means, graphic, electronic, or mechanical, including photocopying, recording, taping or by any information storage retrieval system without the written permission of the author except in the case of brief quotations embodied in critical articles and reviews.

WestBow Press books may be ordered through booksellers or by contacting:

WestBow Press
A Division of Thomas Nelson & Zondervan
1663 Liberty Drive
Bloomington, IN 47403
www.westbowpress.com
844-714-3454

Because of the dynamic nature of the Internet, any web addresses or links contained in this book may have changed since publication and may no longer be valid. The views expressed in this work are solely those of the author and do not necessarily reflect the views of the publisher, and the publisher hereby disclaims any responsibility for them.

Any people depicted in stock imagery provided by Getty Images are models,
and such images are being used for illustrative purposes only.
Certain stock imagery © Getty Images.

ISBN: 979-8-3850-0527-7 (sc)
ISBN: 979-8-3850-0528-4 (e)

Print information available on the last page.

WestBow Press rev. date: 11/15/2024

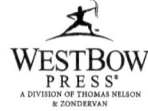

Introduction

Welcome to my first colouring book- Drawn to Dwell, adult colouring. My name is Rebecca Johnston and my prayer is over the next sixty pages that you would be able to see these verses afresh. I would encourage you to look up these verses and read a little bit of the verses around them to get the full context. May God encourage, inspire, and give you hope as you colour.

Feel free to test your art mediums on the bottom of this page and share your coloured pages with me on Instagram @drawn_to_dwell

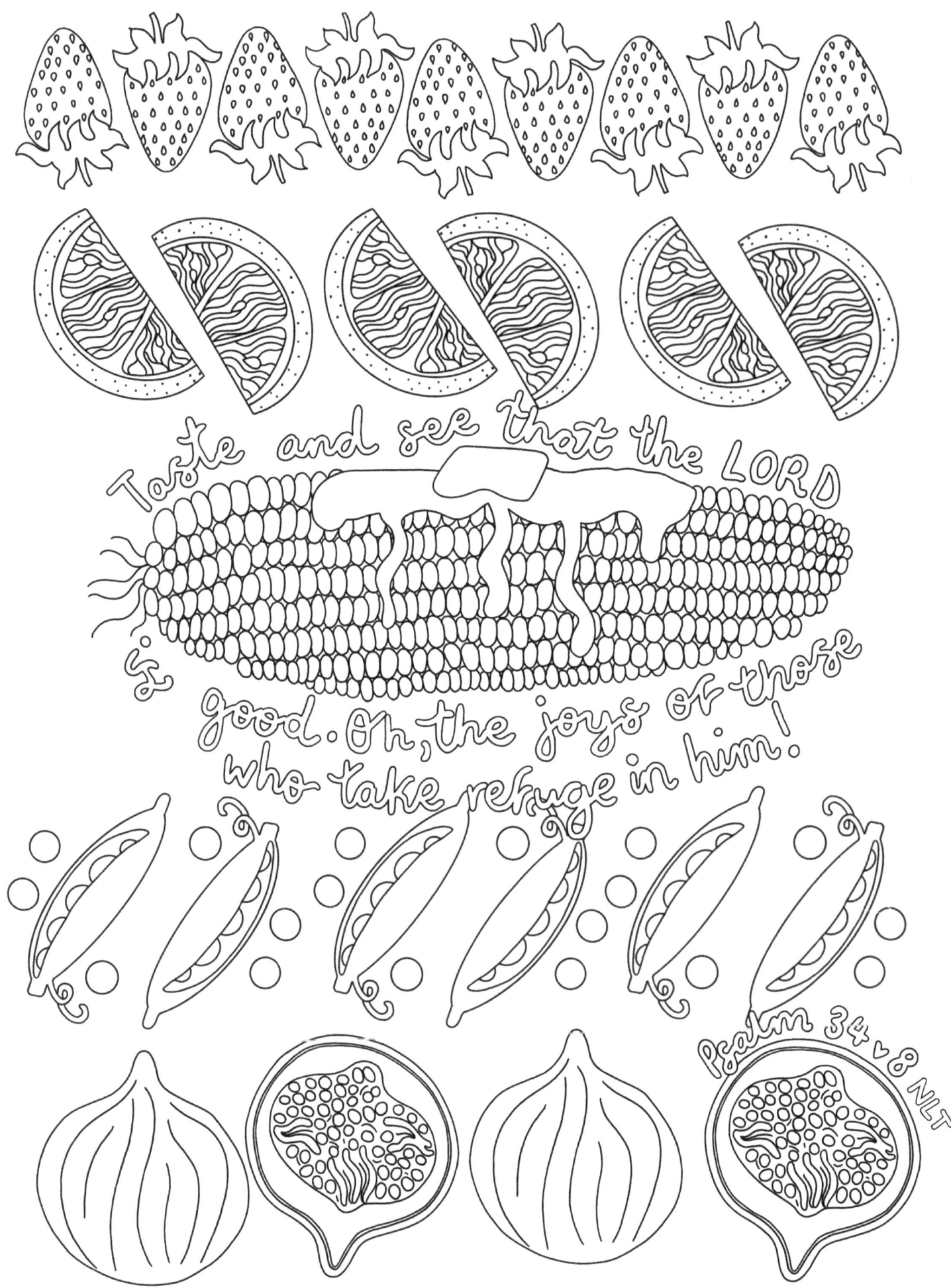

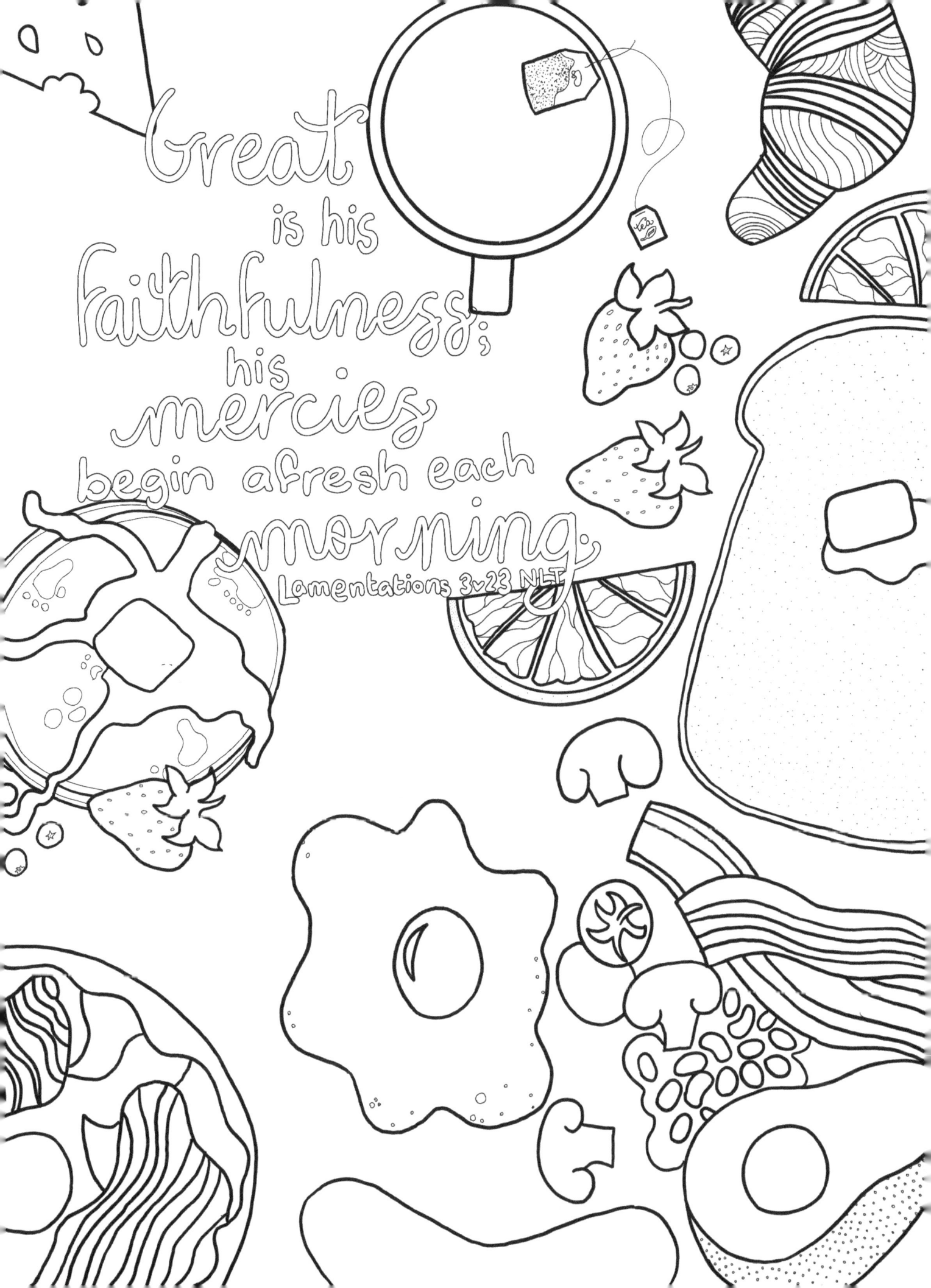

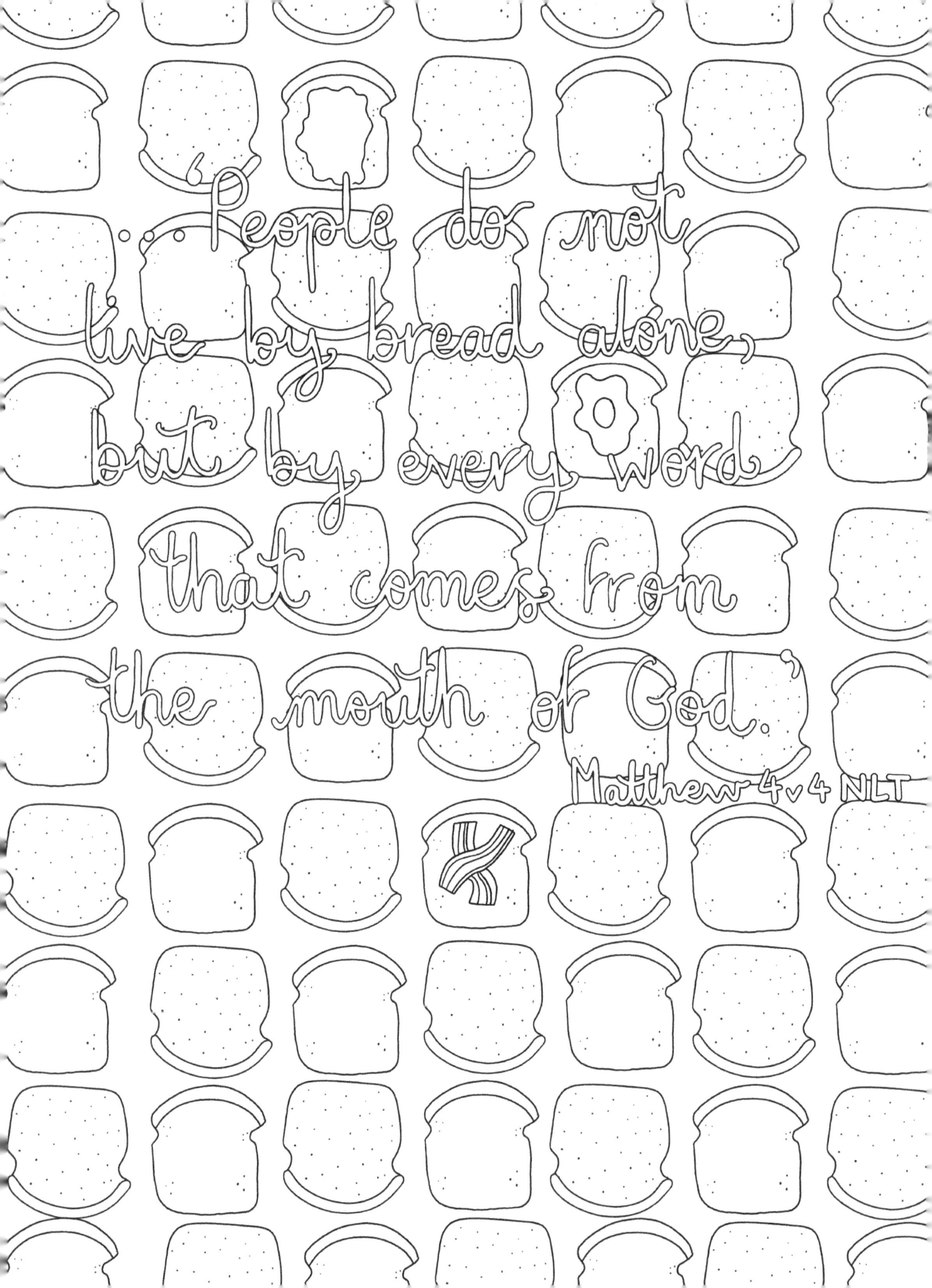

"People do not live by bread alone, but by every word that comes from the mouth of God."
Matthew 4v4 NLT

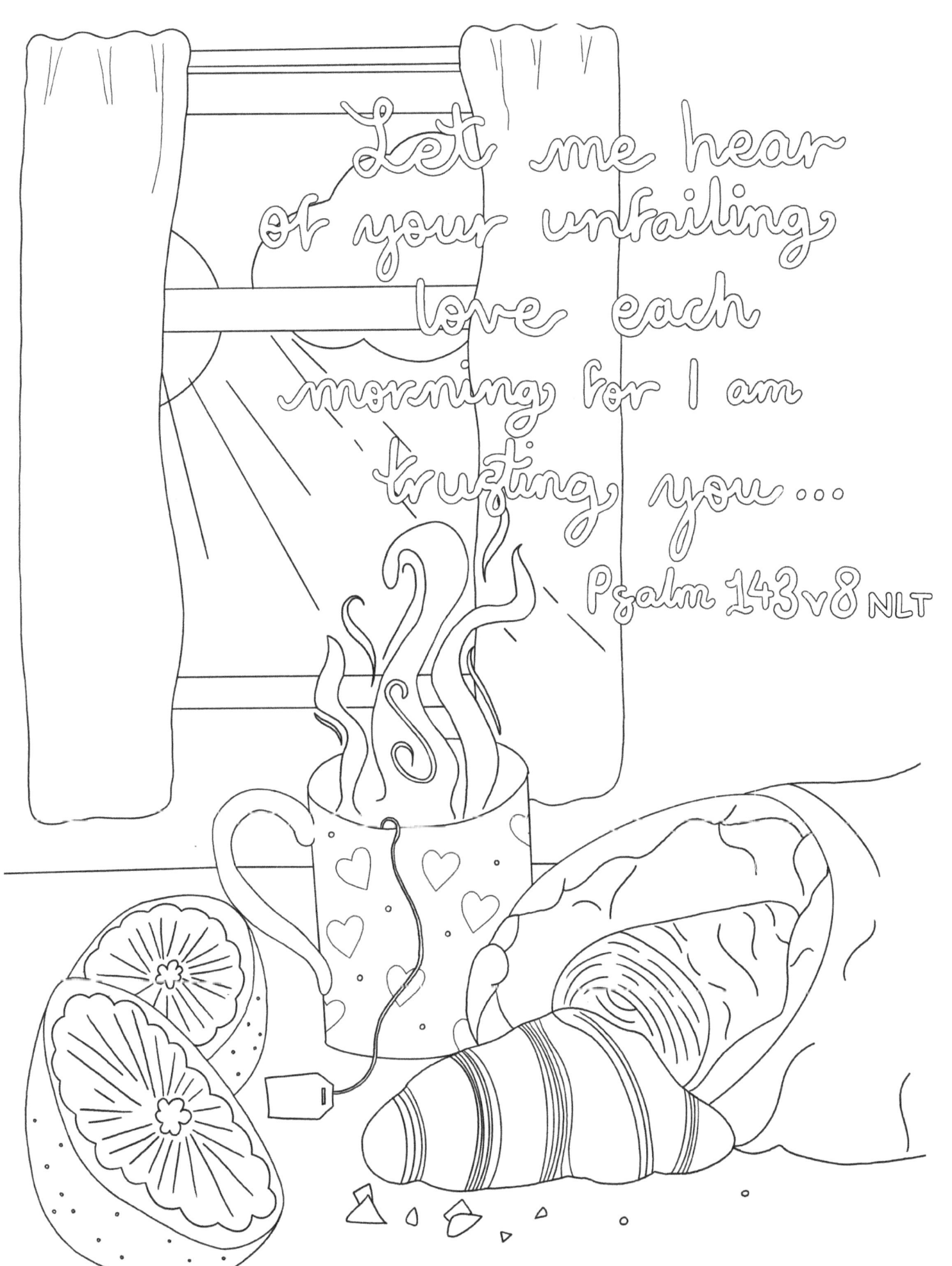

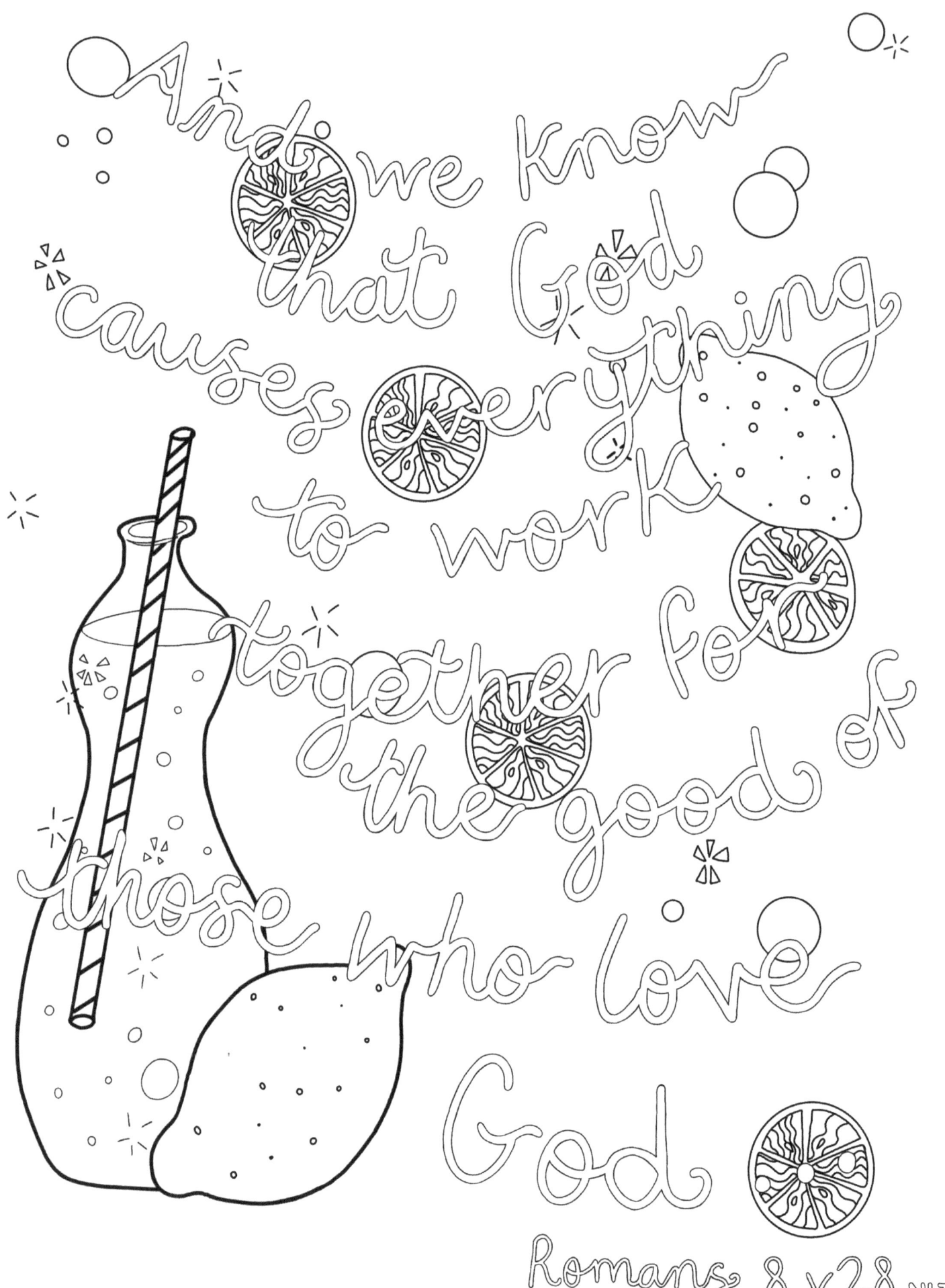

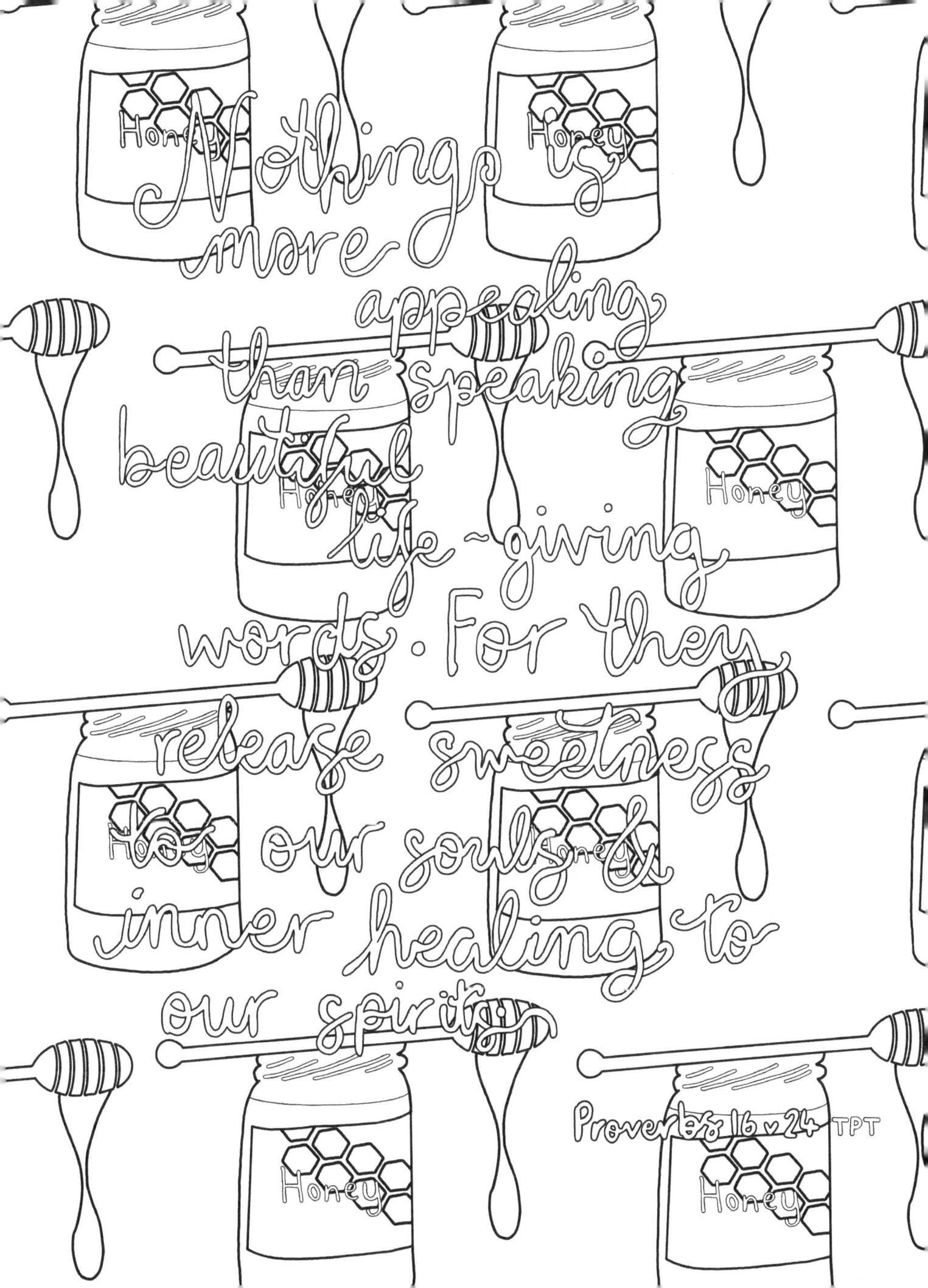

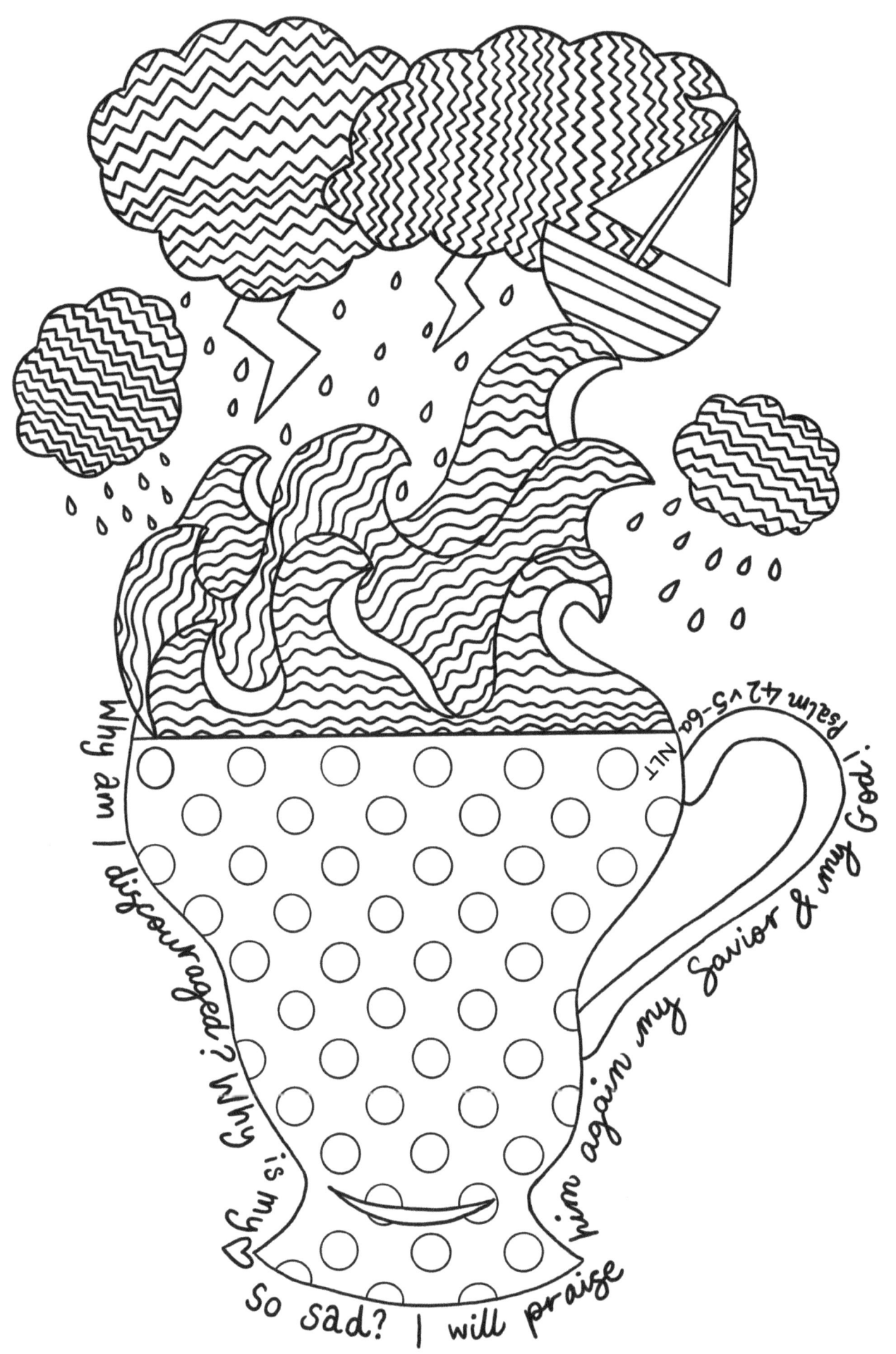

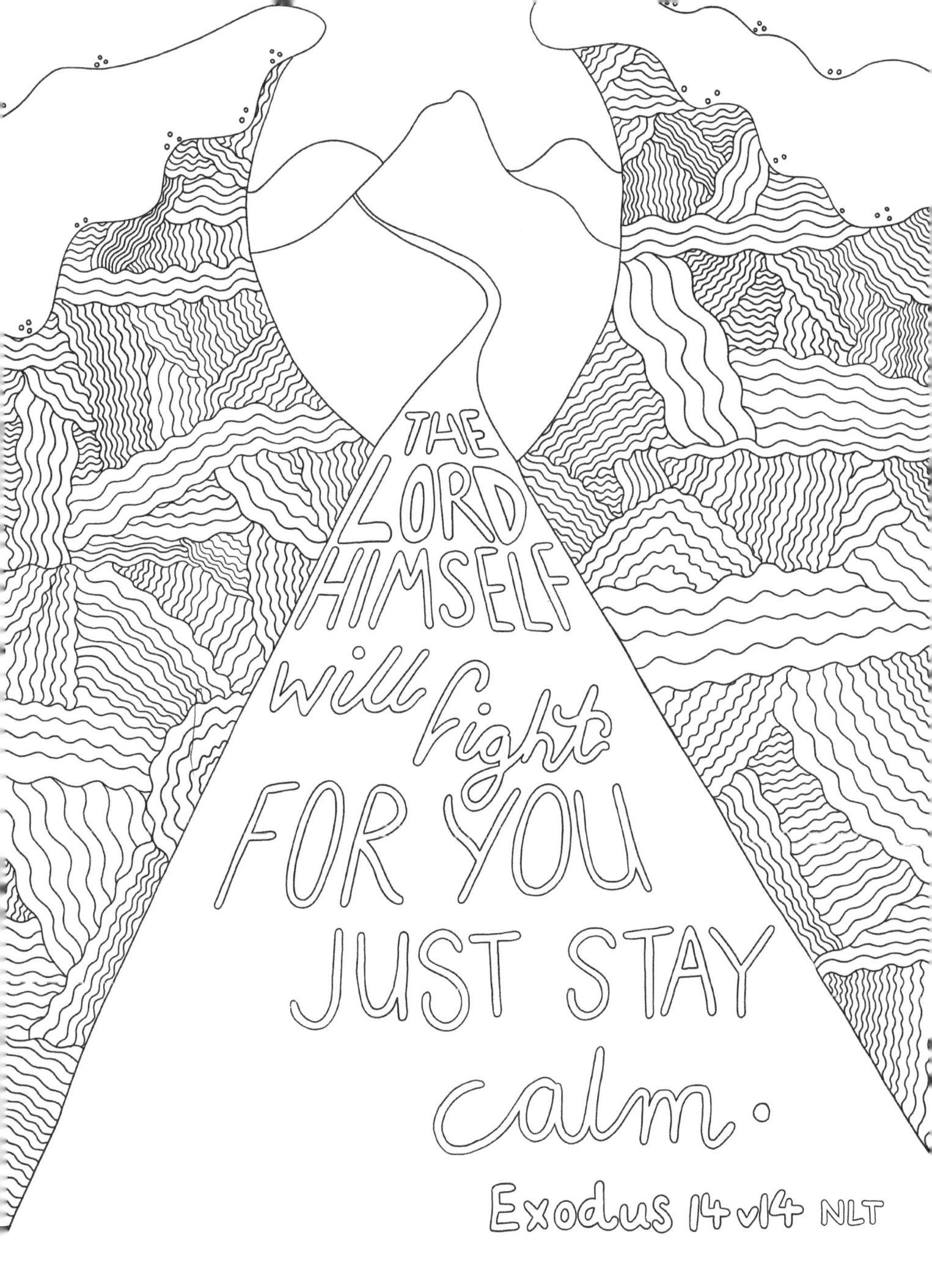

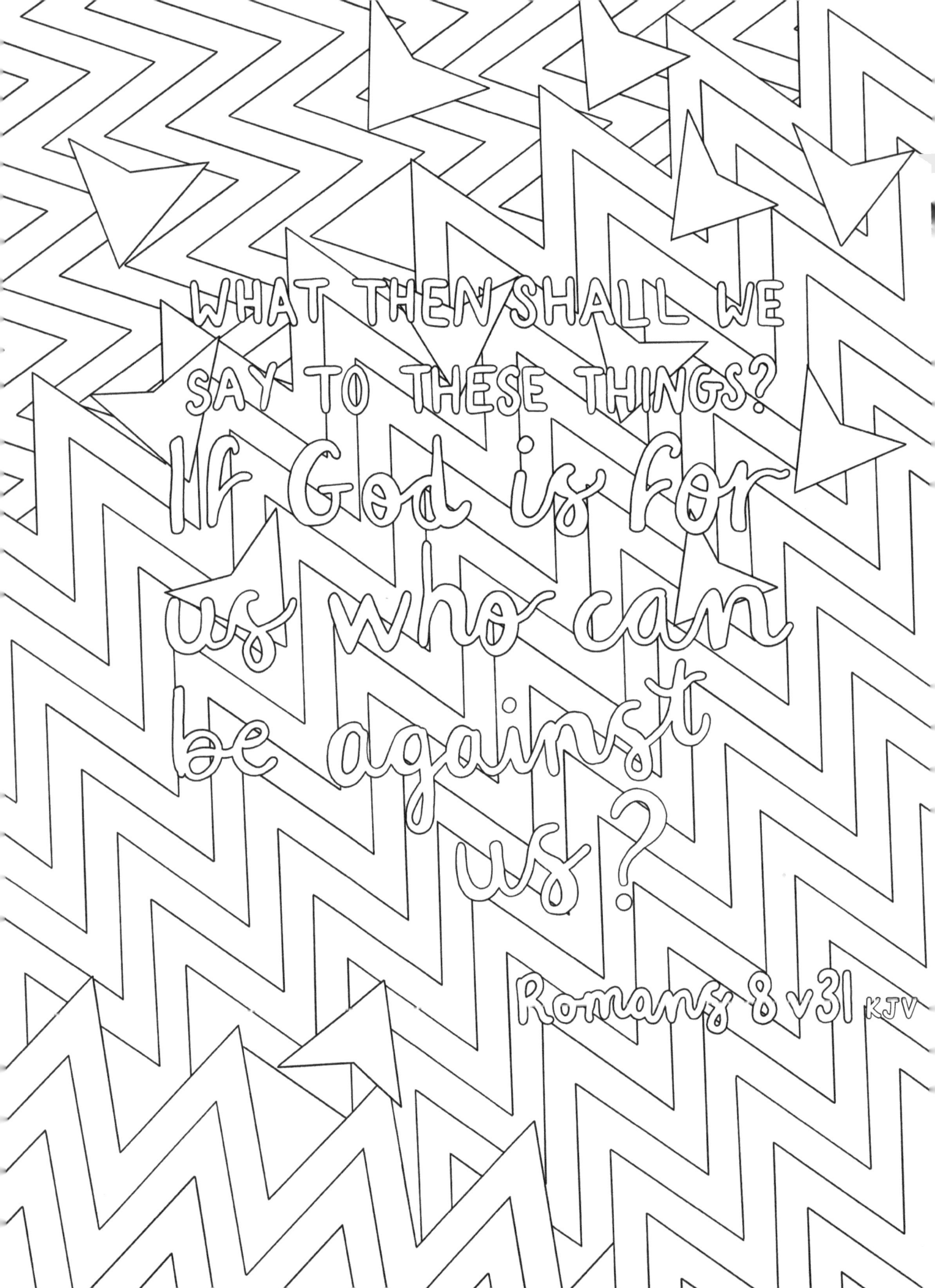

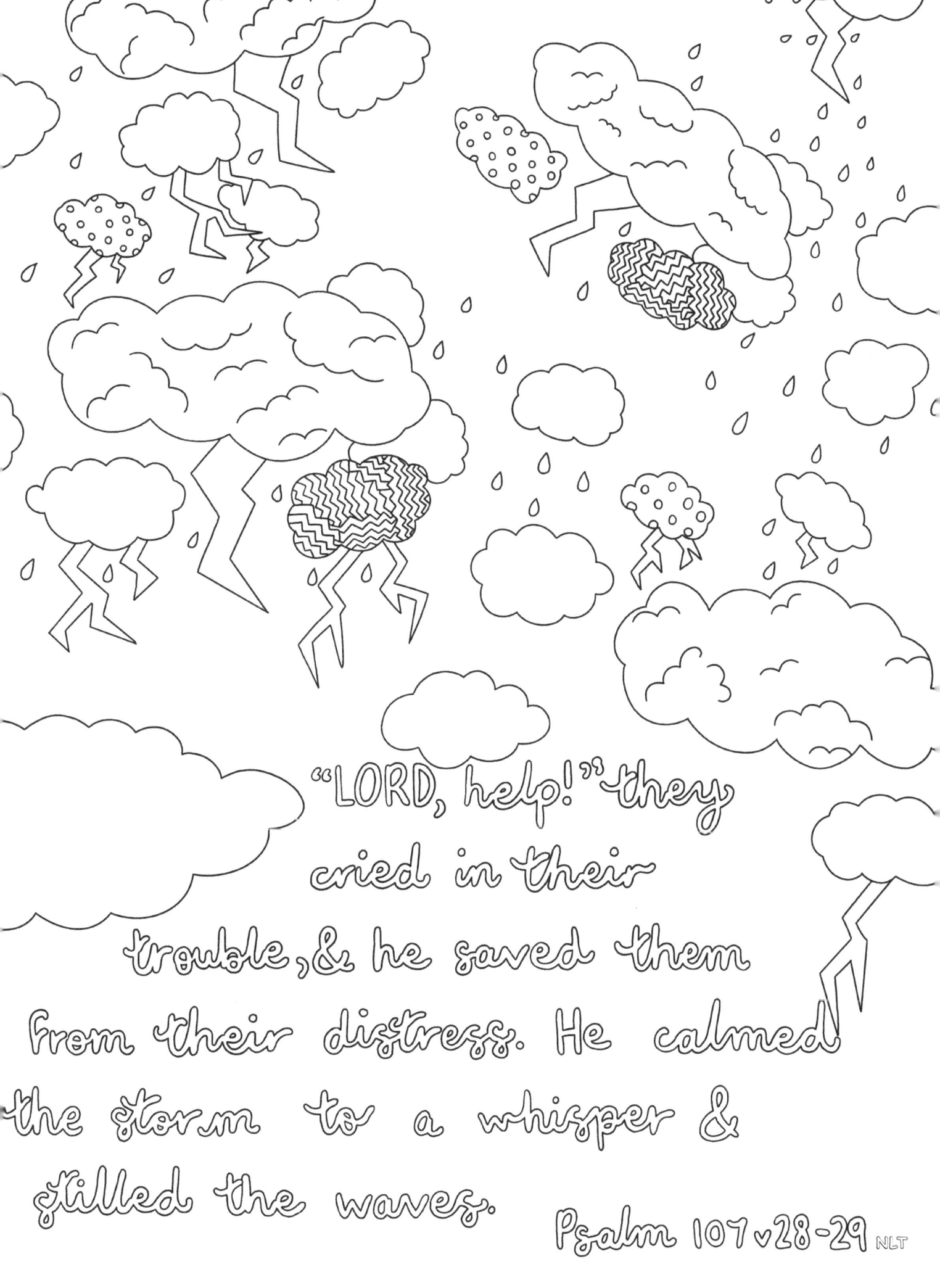

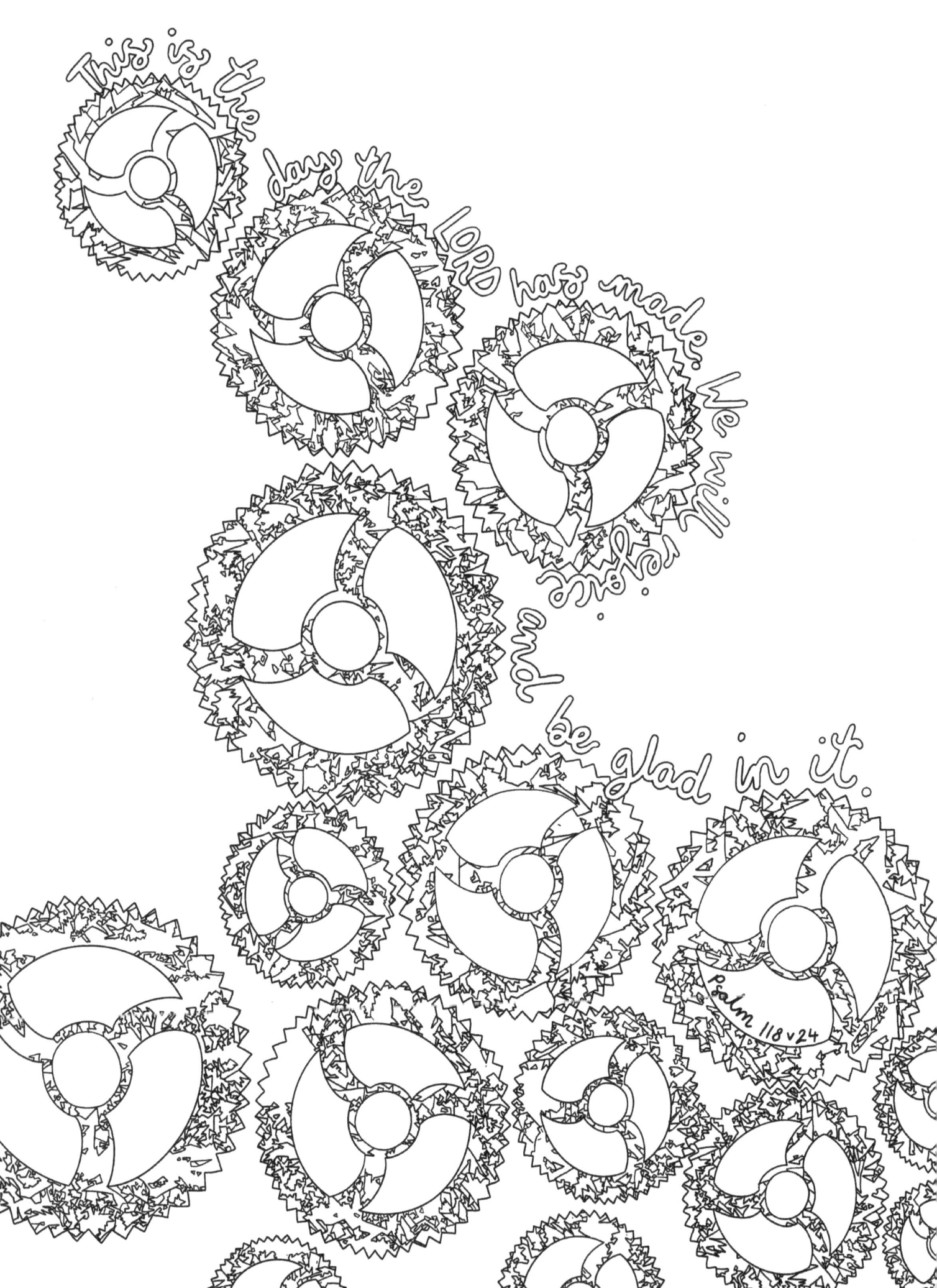

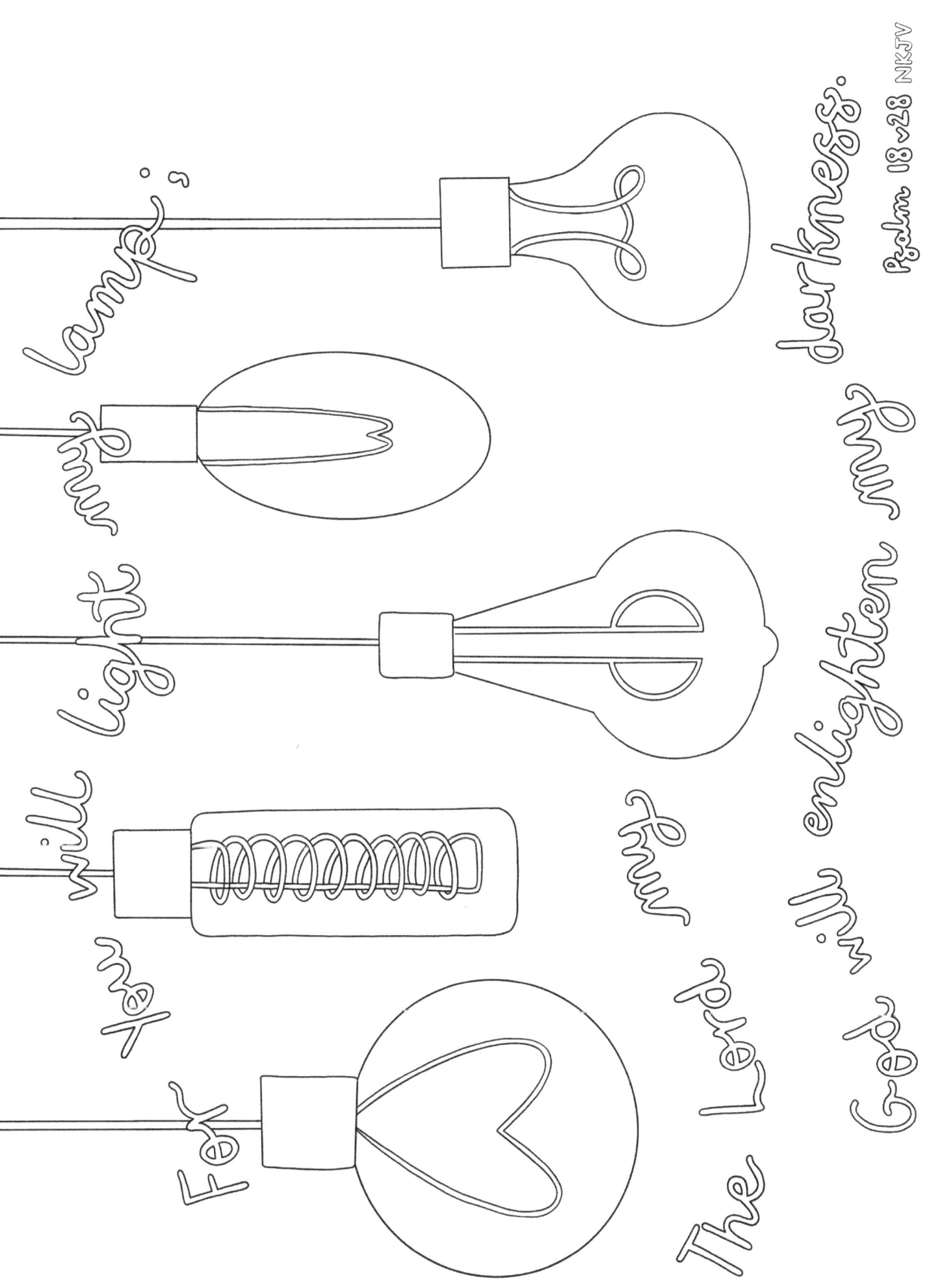

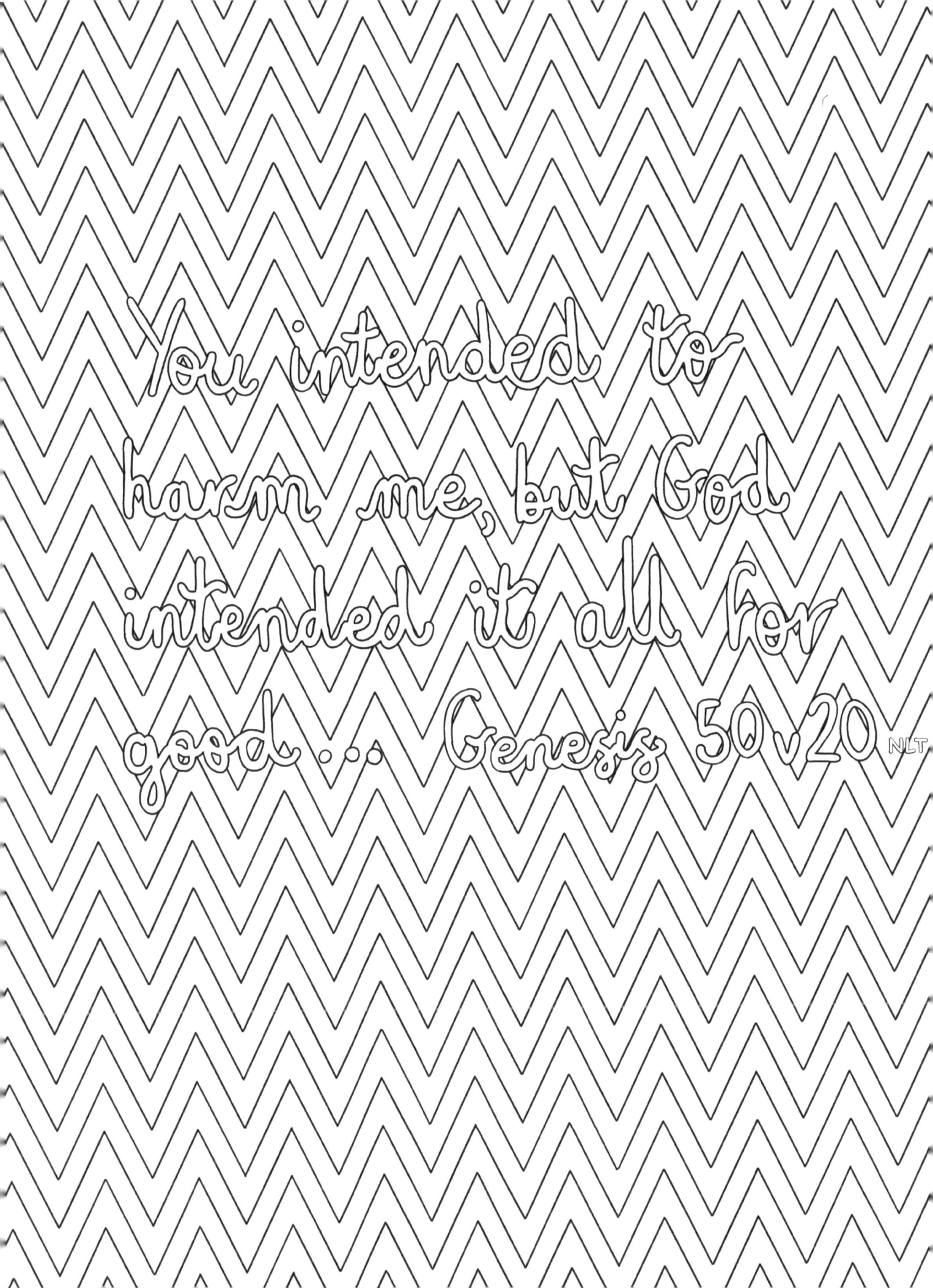

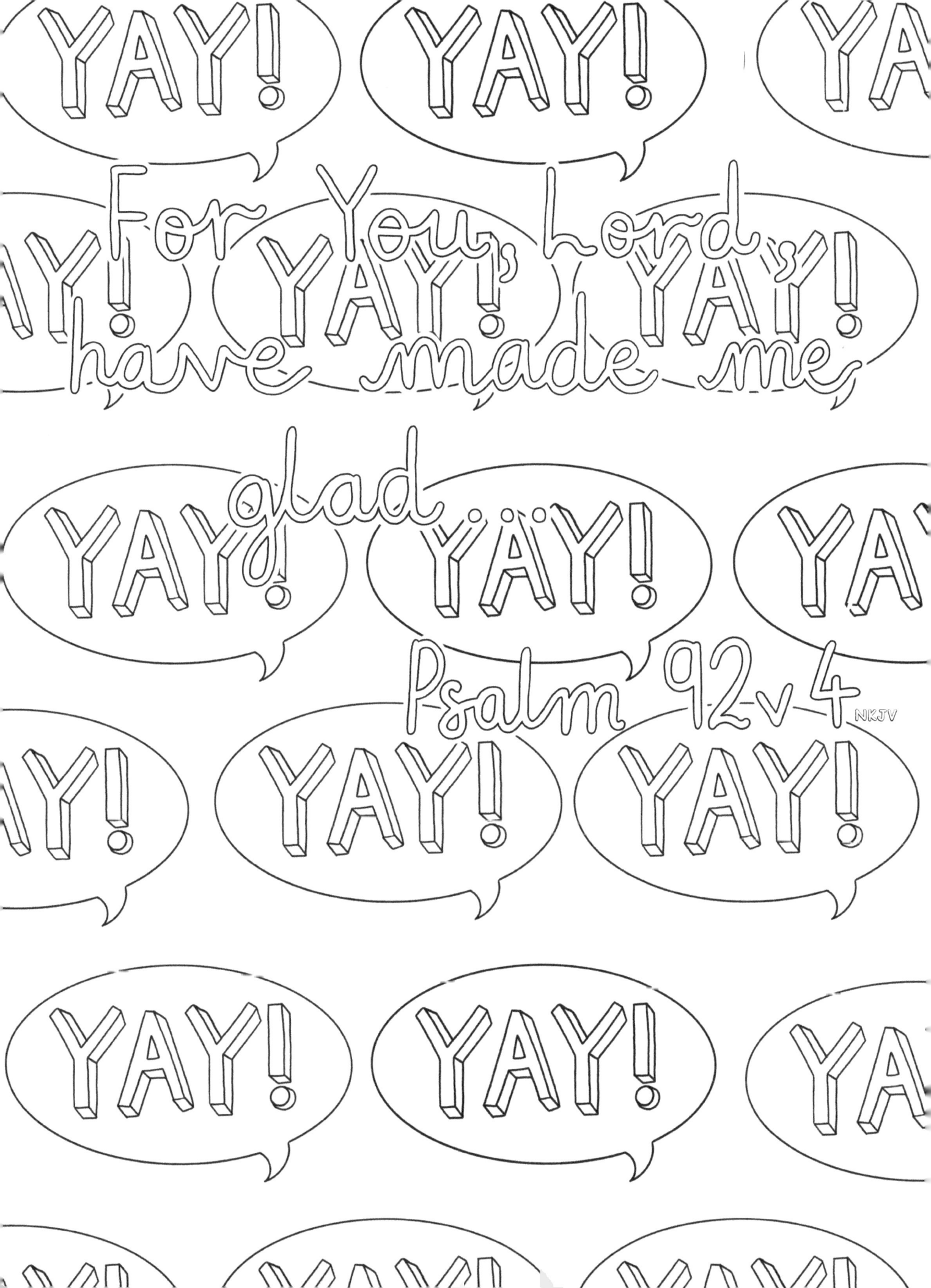

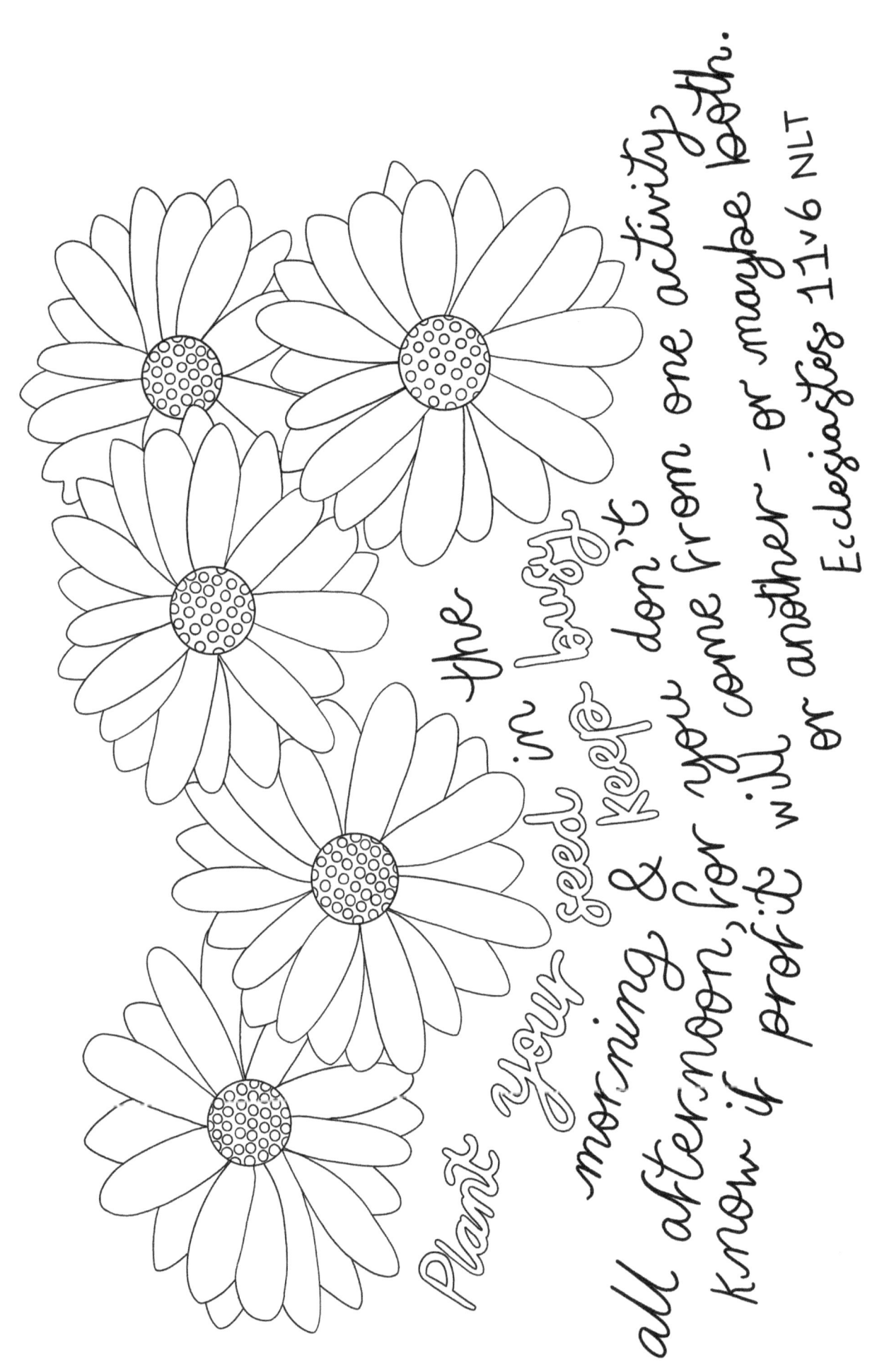

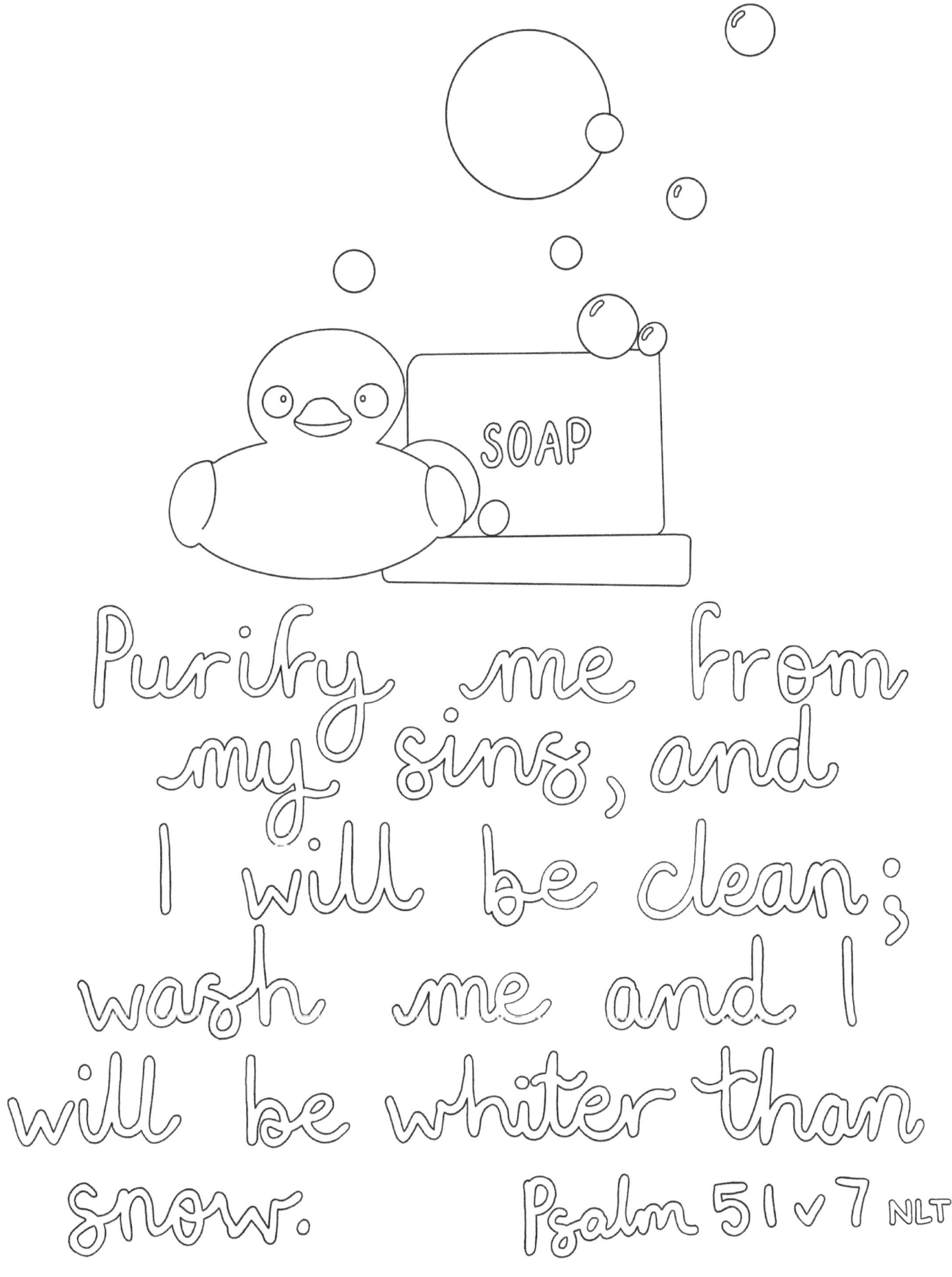

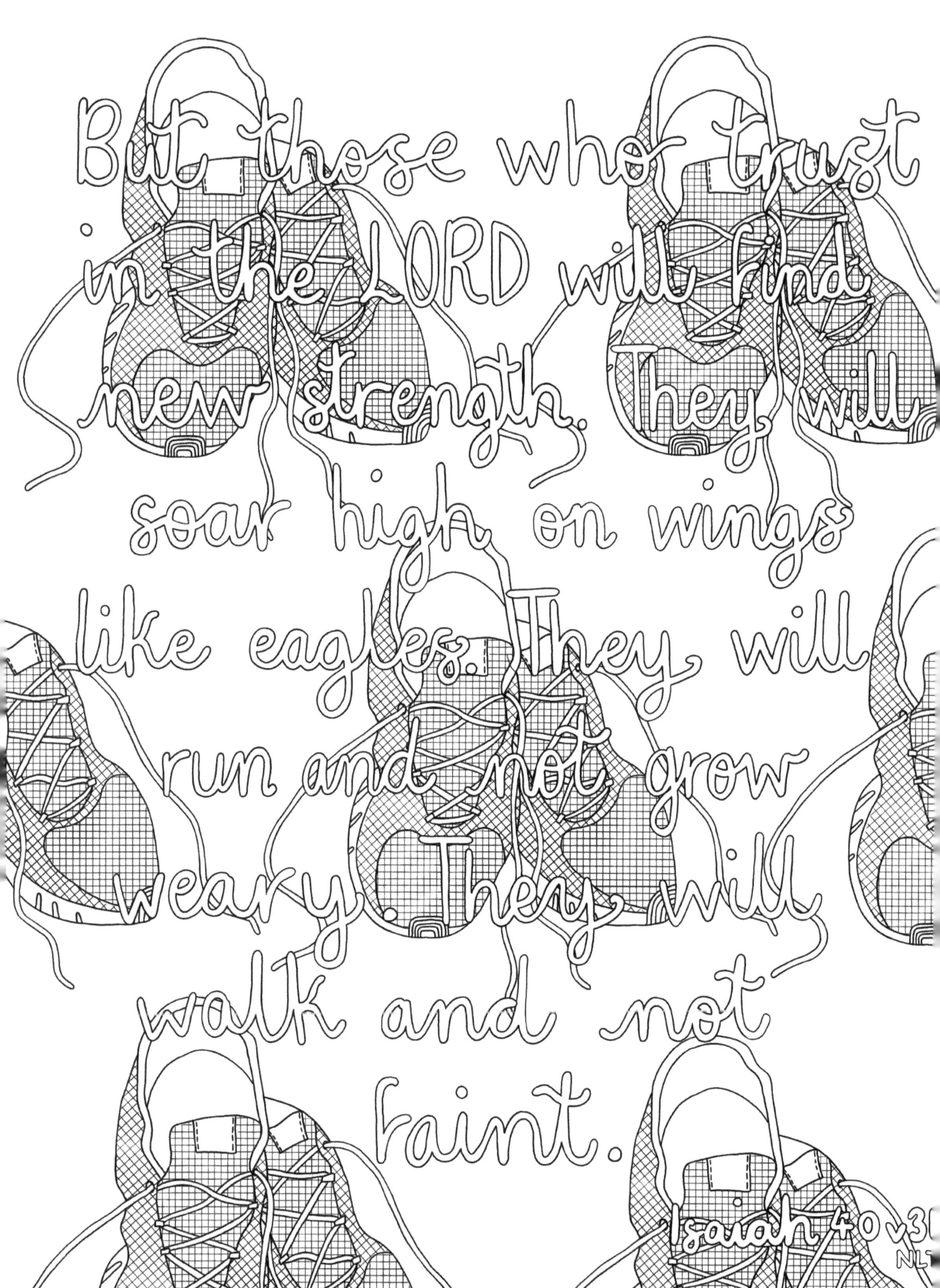

He lifted me out of the pit of despair, out of the mud and mire. He set my feet on solid ground and steadied me as I walked along.

Psalm 40v2 NLT

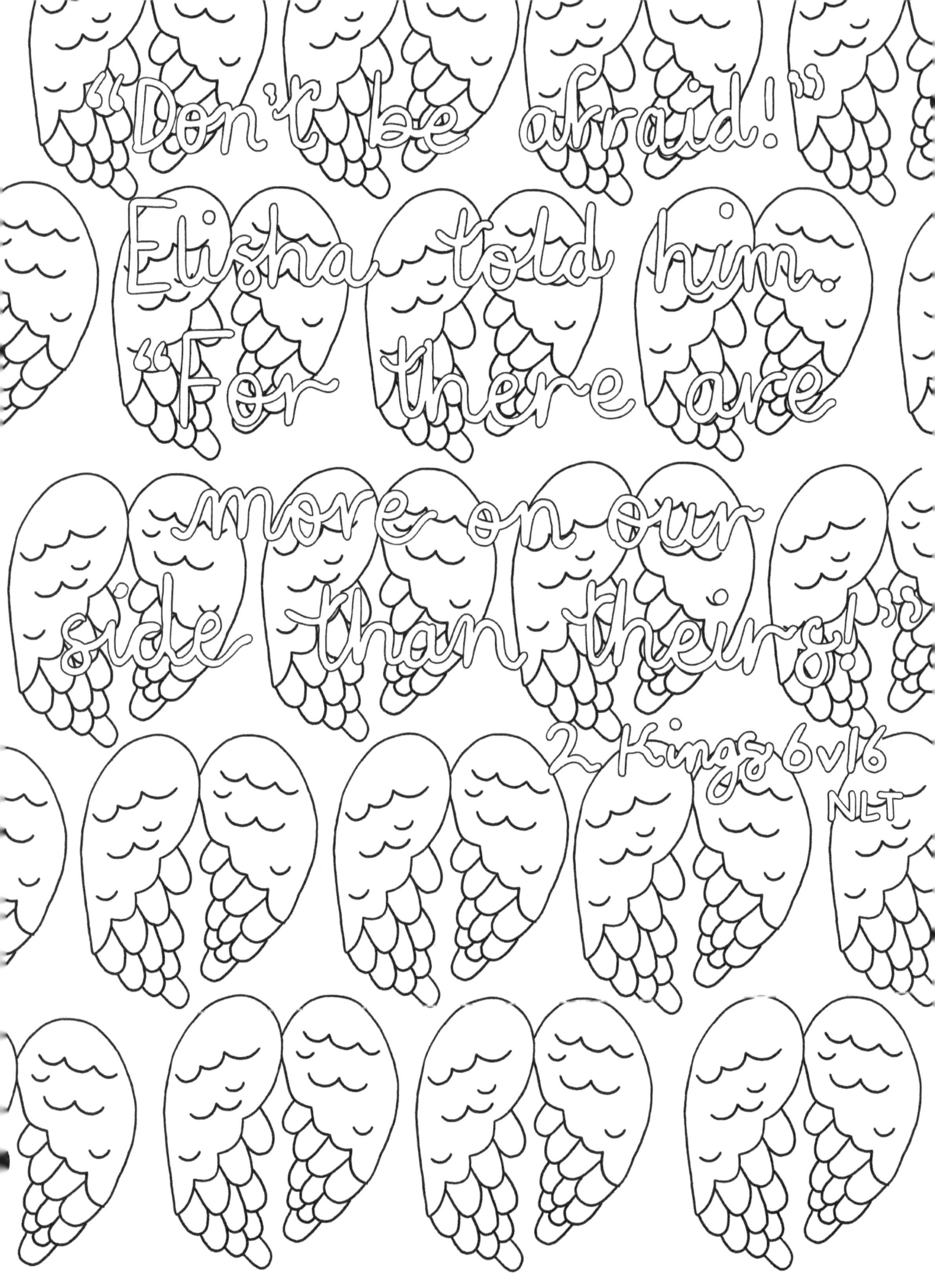

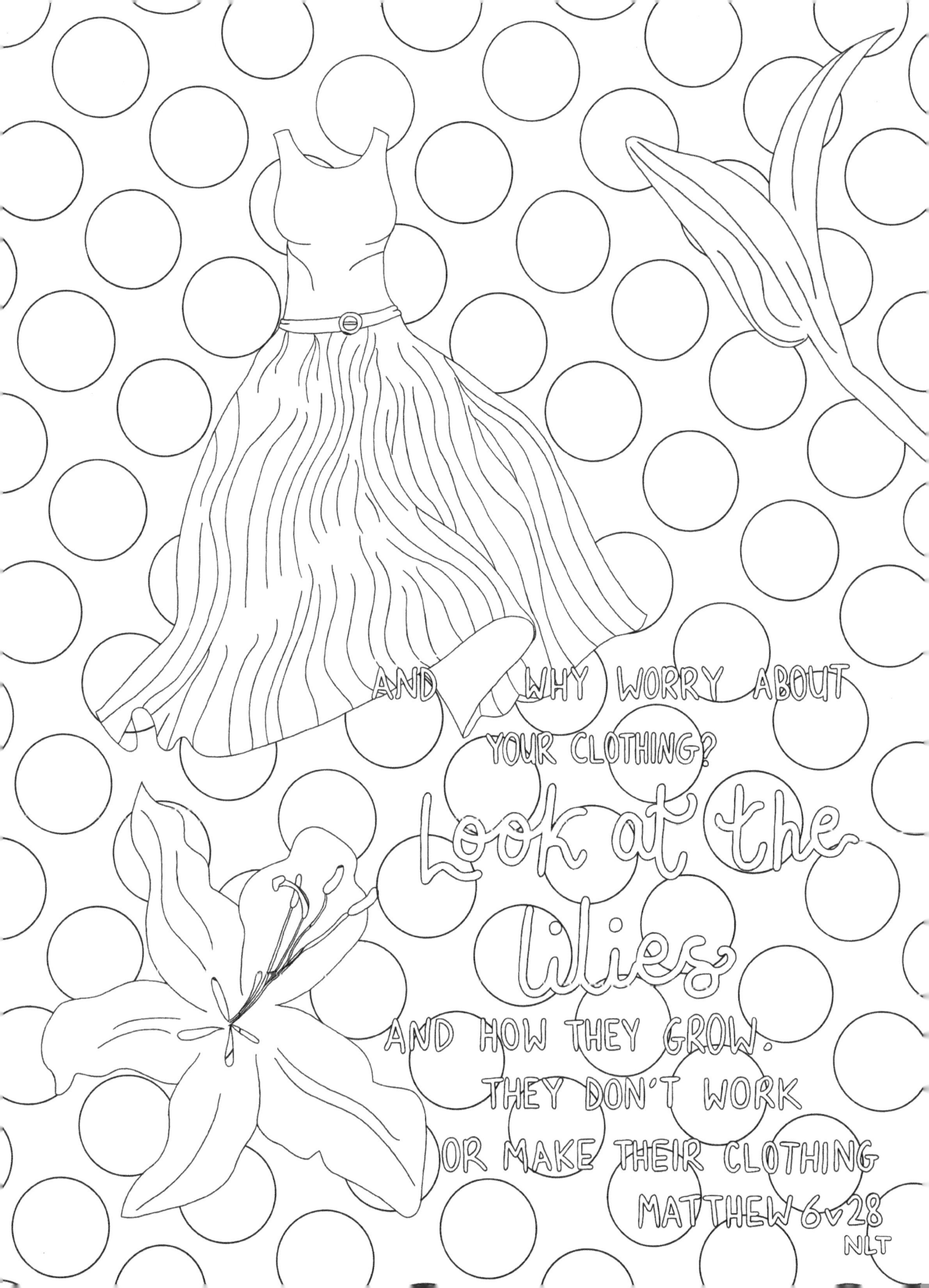

You can go to bed without fear; you will lie down & sleep soundly.

Proverbs 3v24 NLT

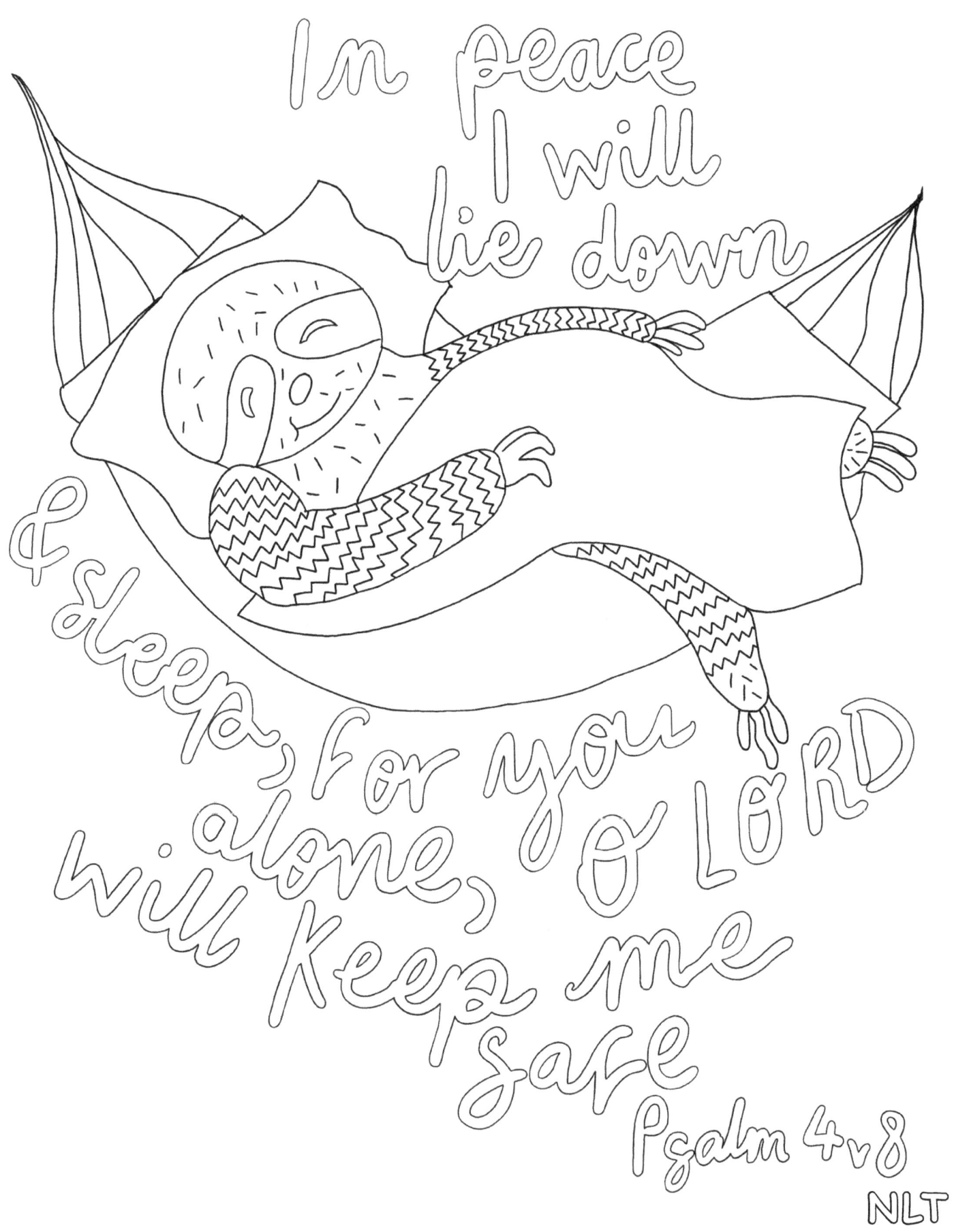

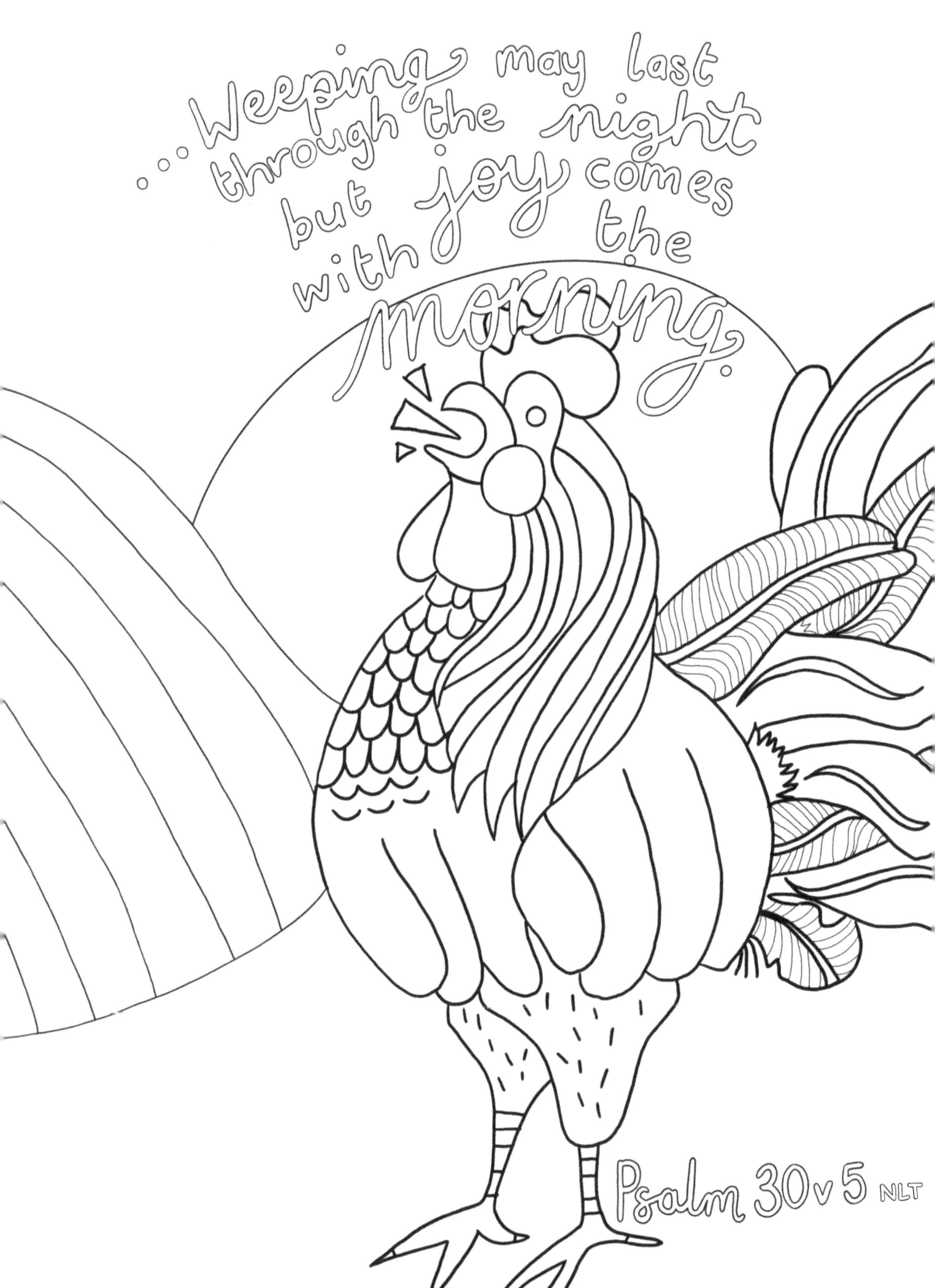

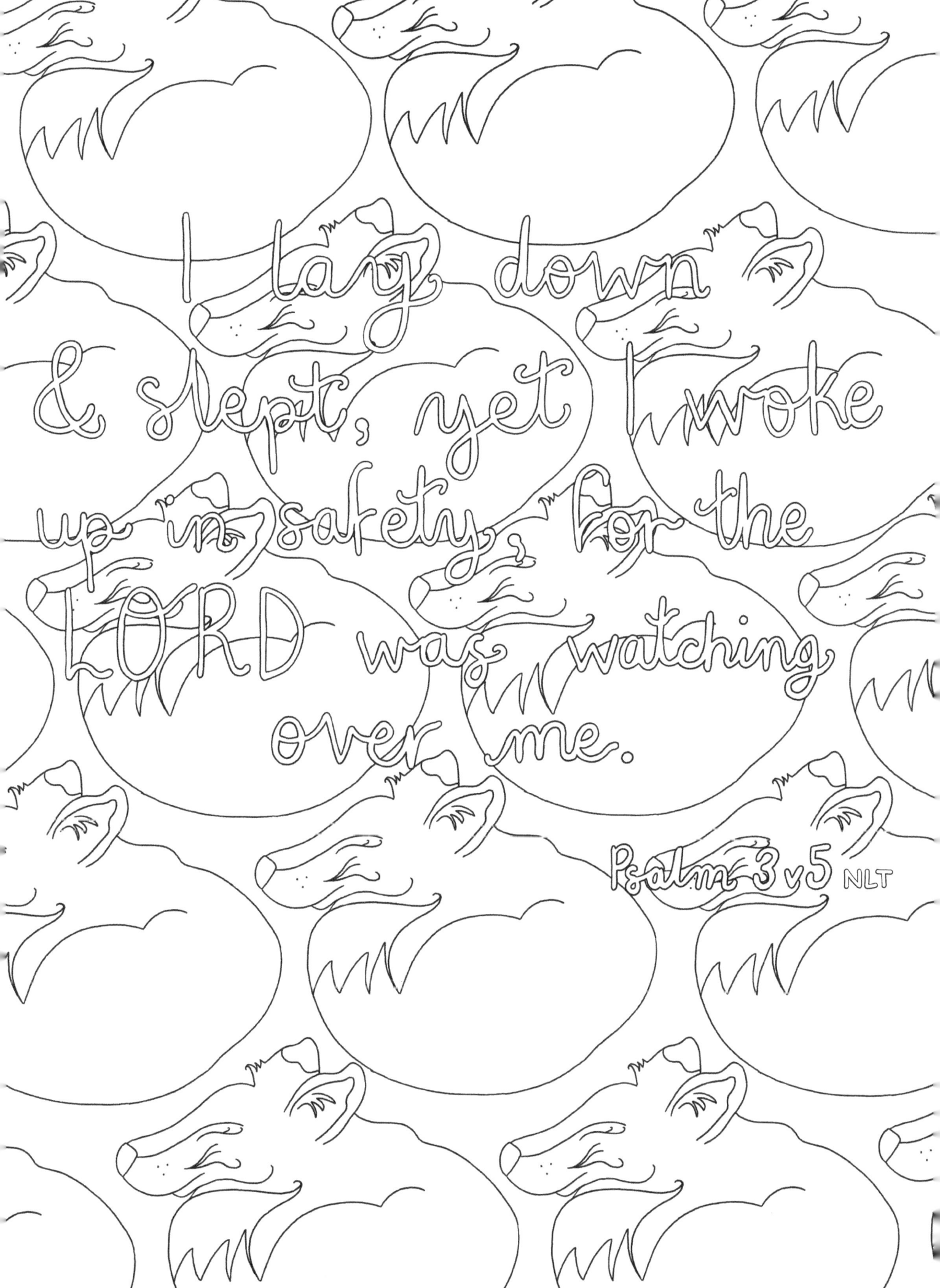

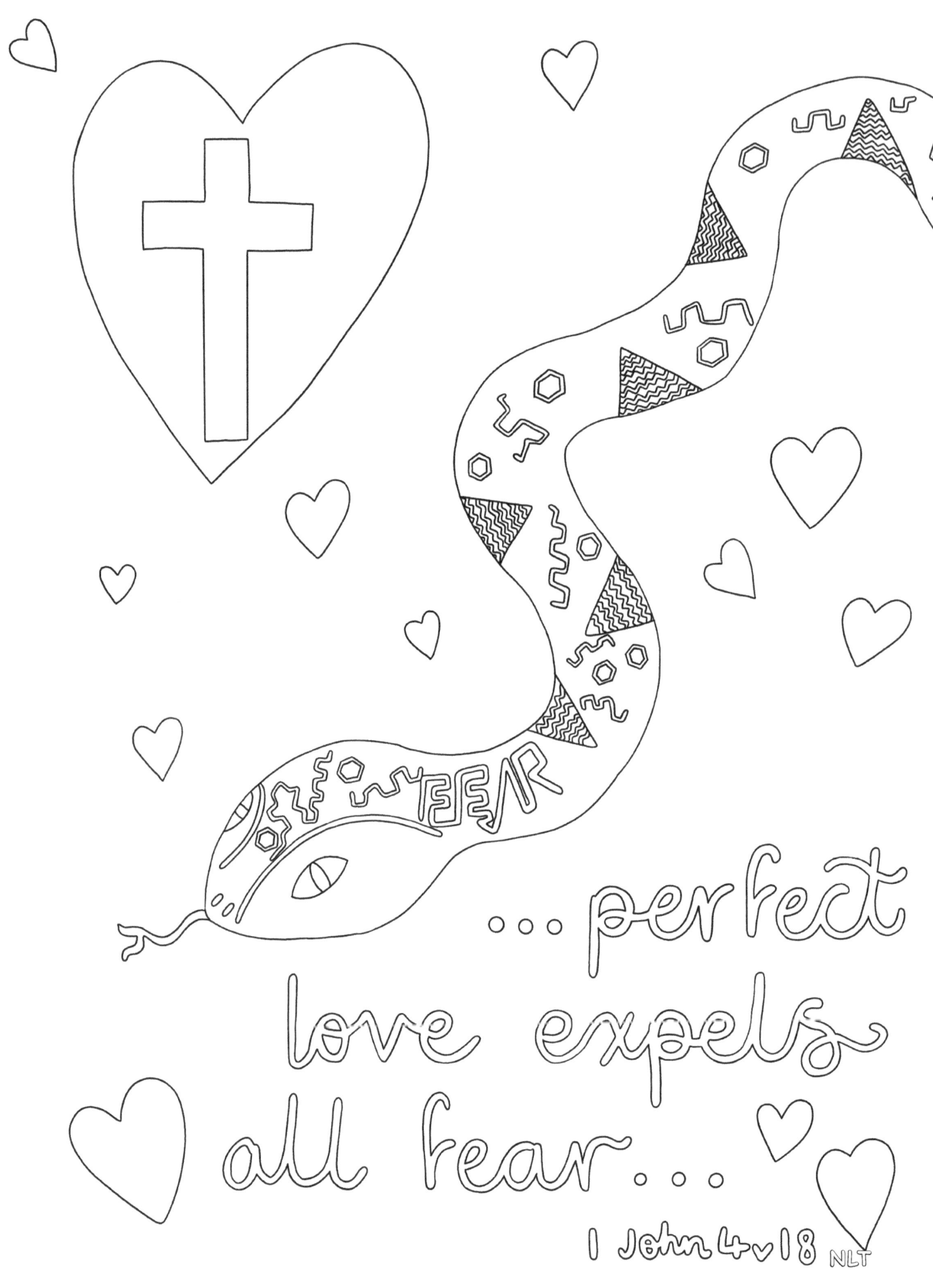

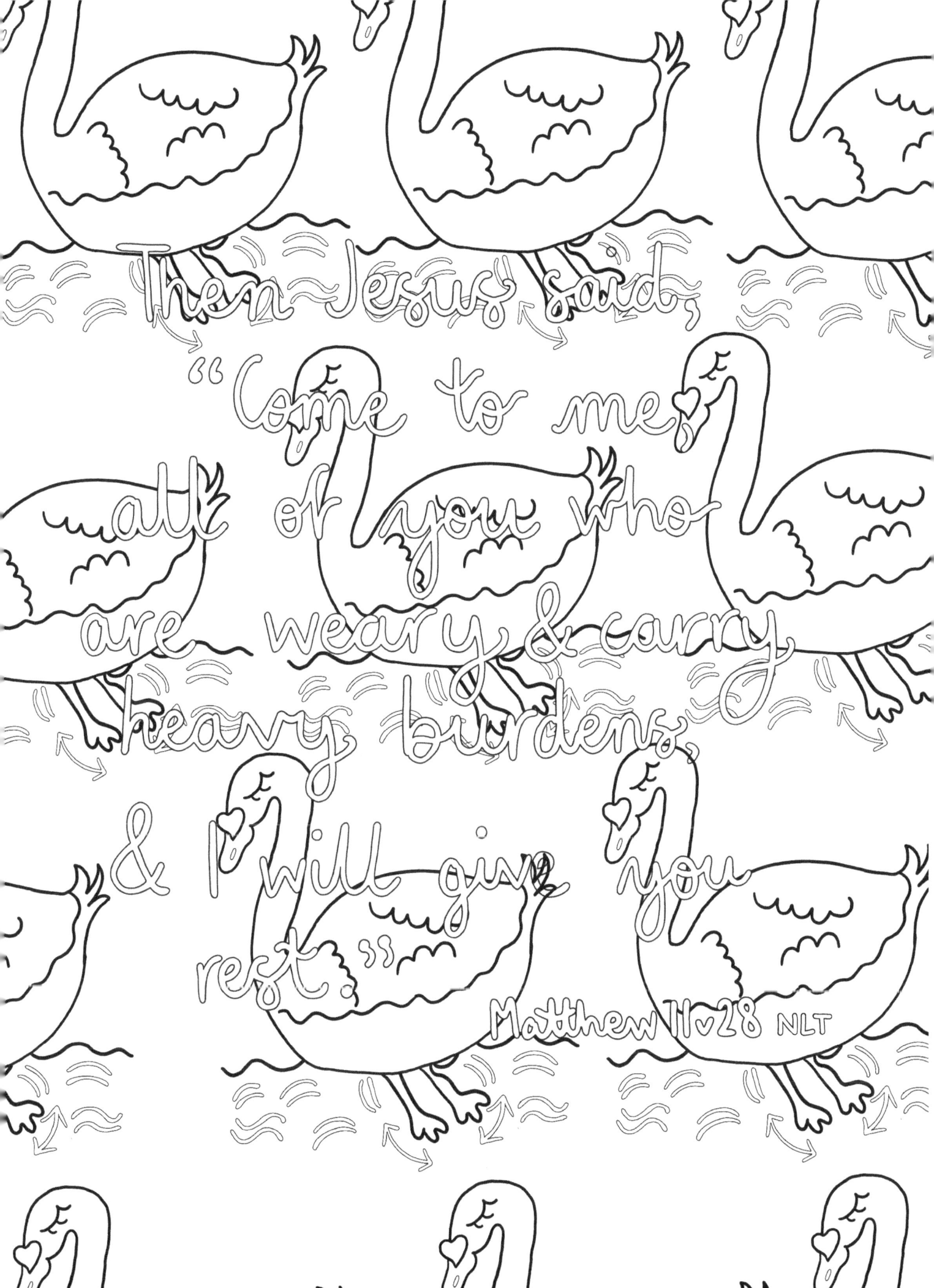

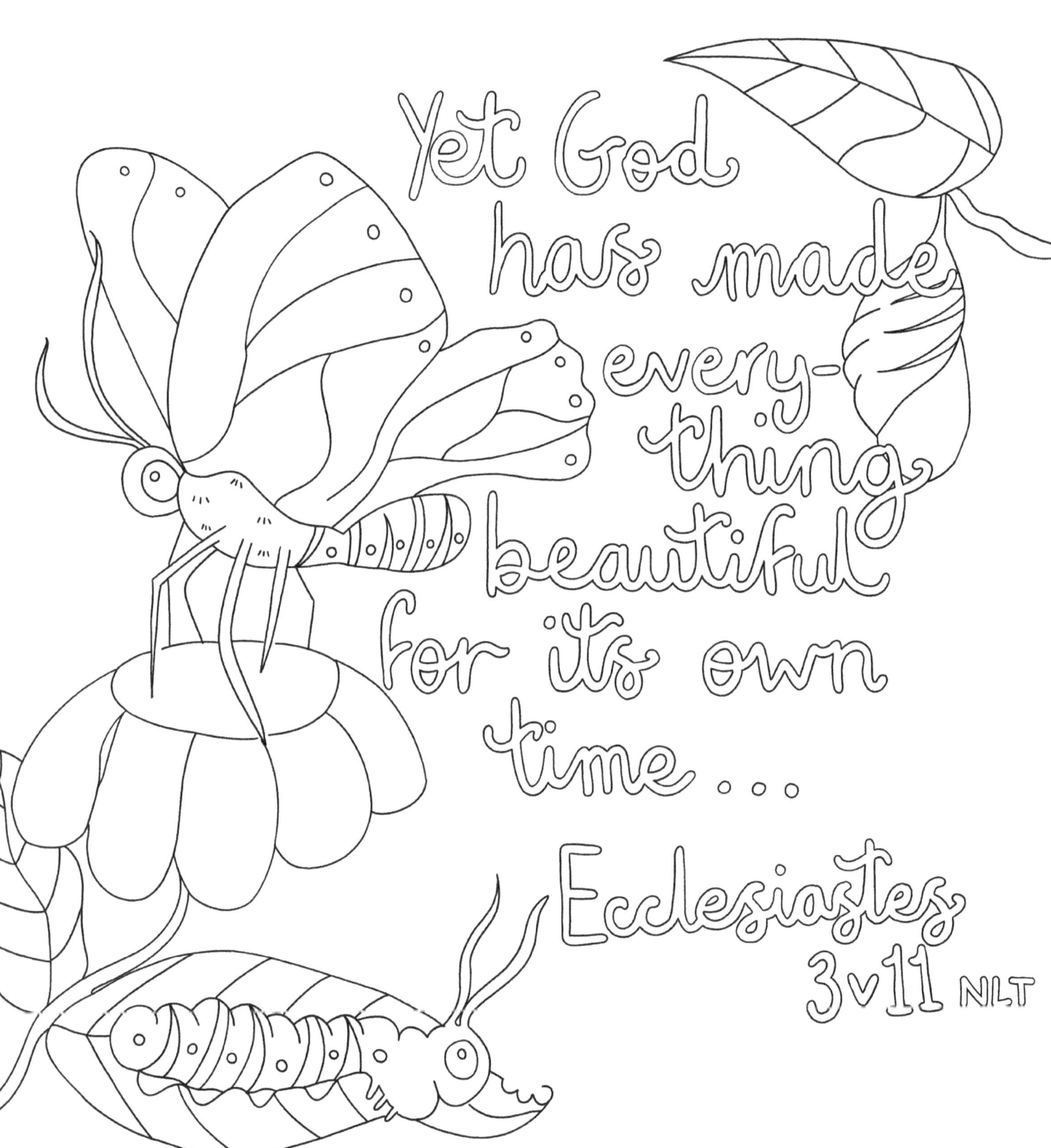

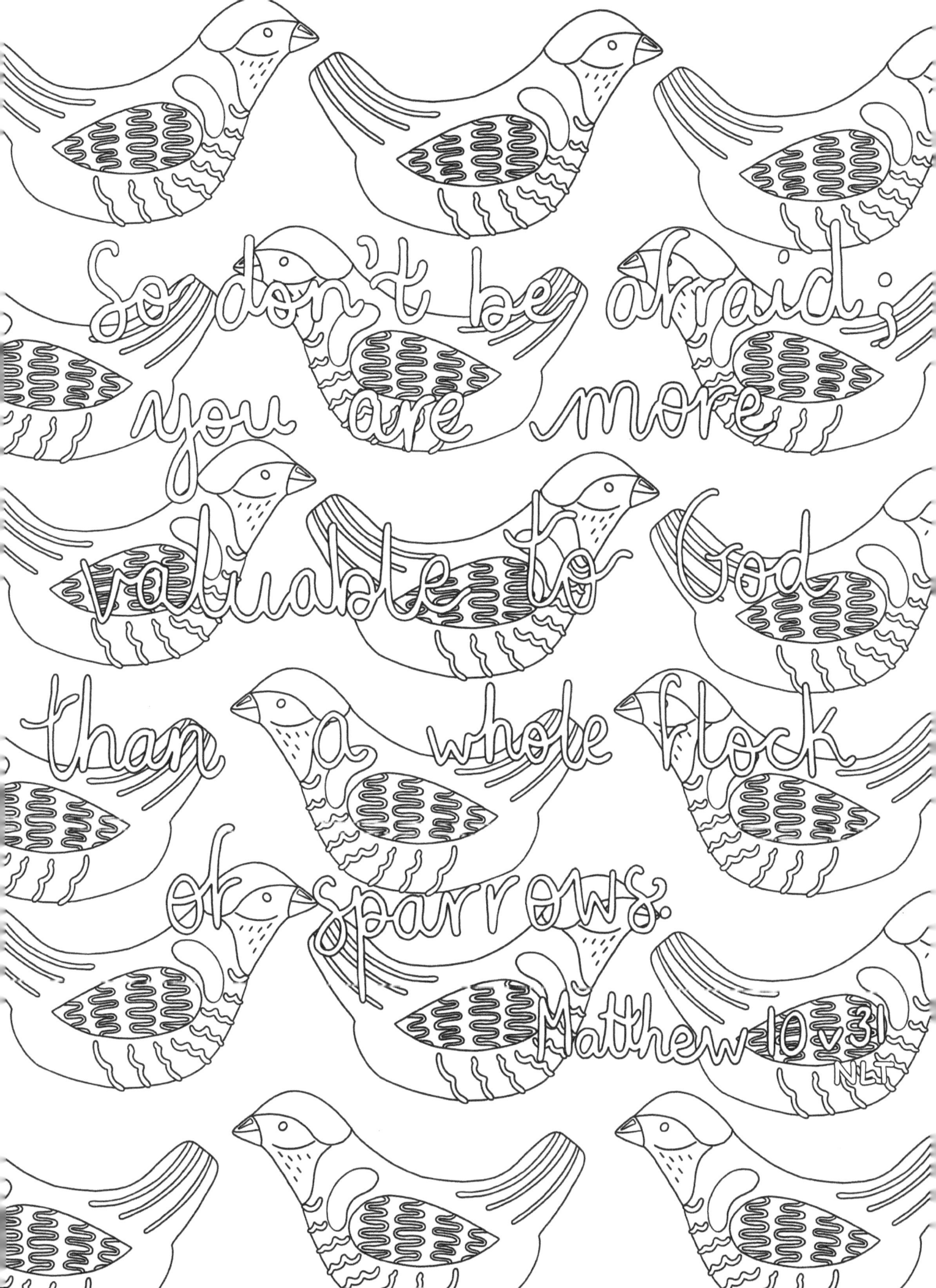

And may you have the power to understand as all God's people should, how wide, how long, how high, and deep his love is.

Ephesians 3v18 NLT

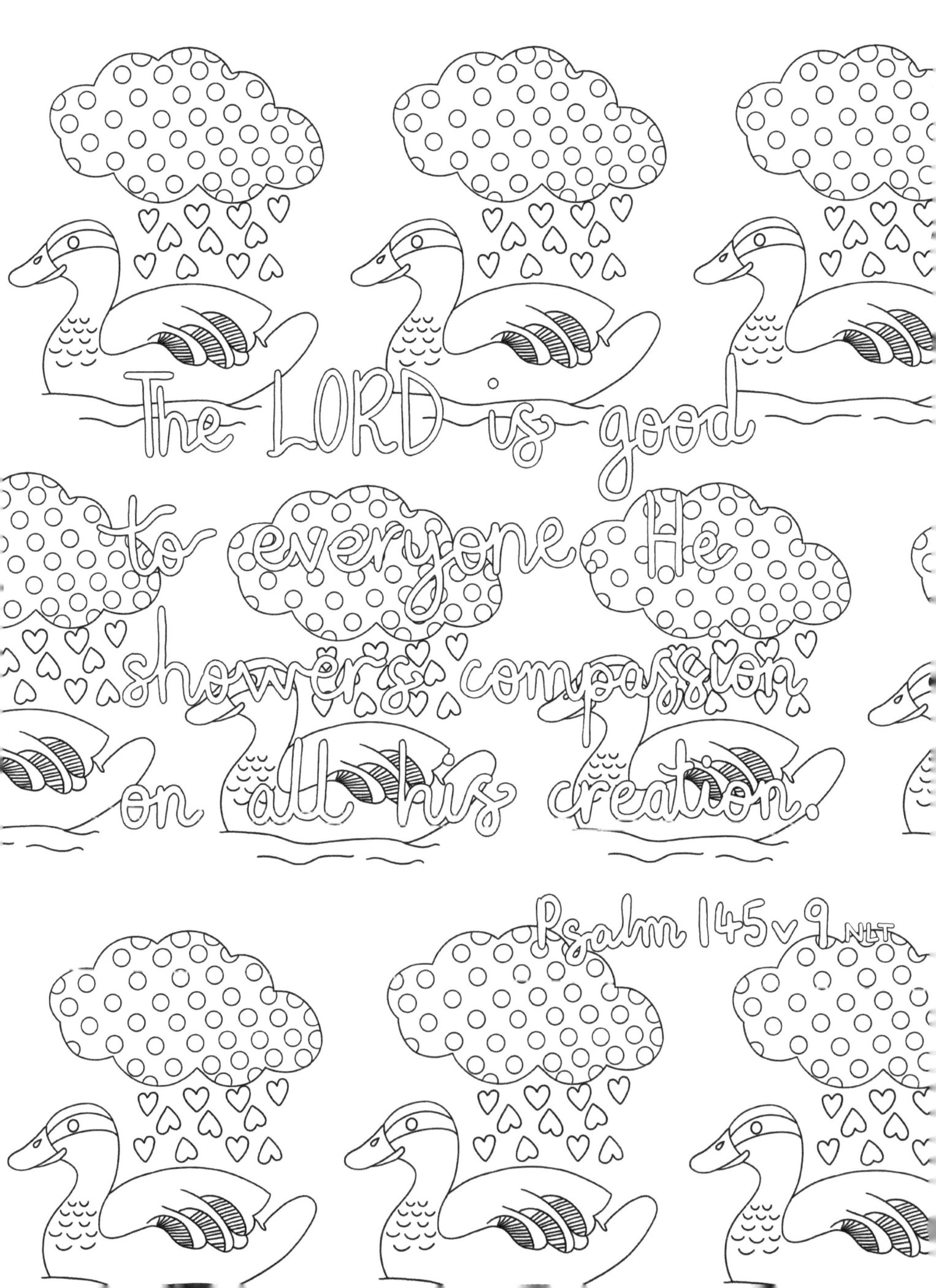

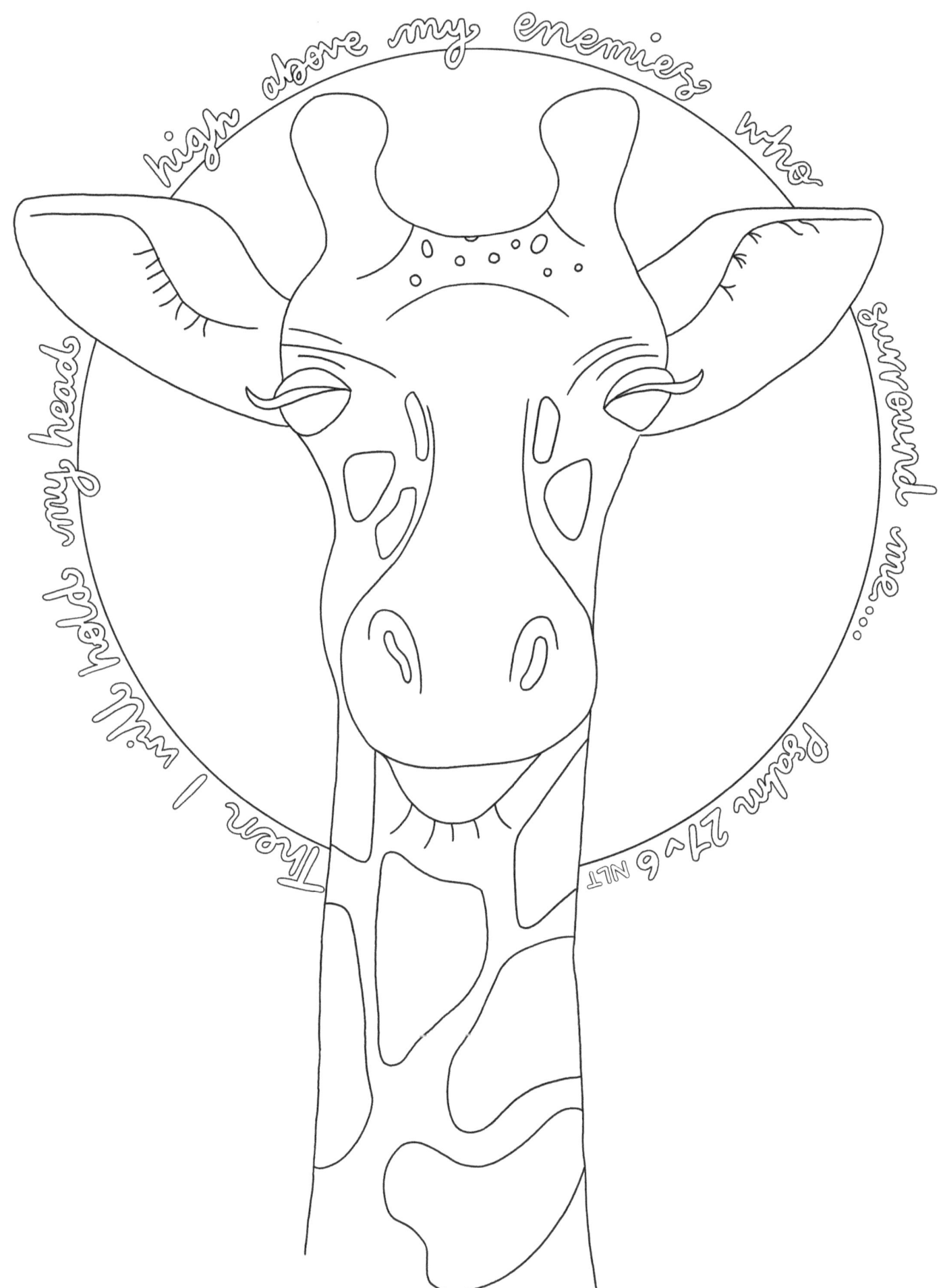

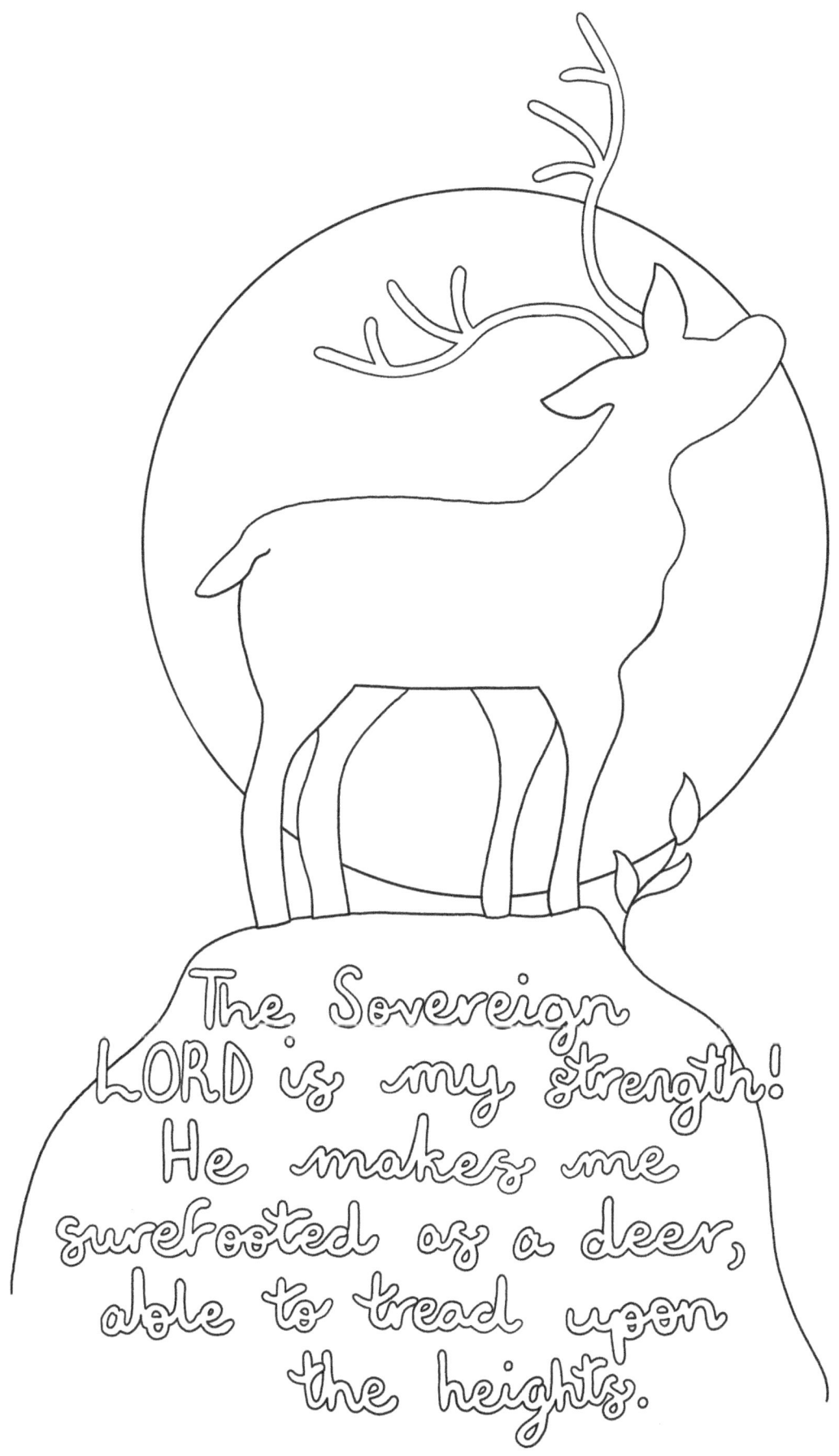

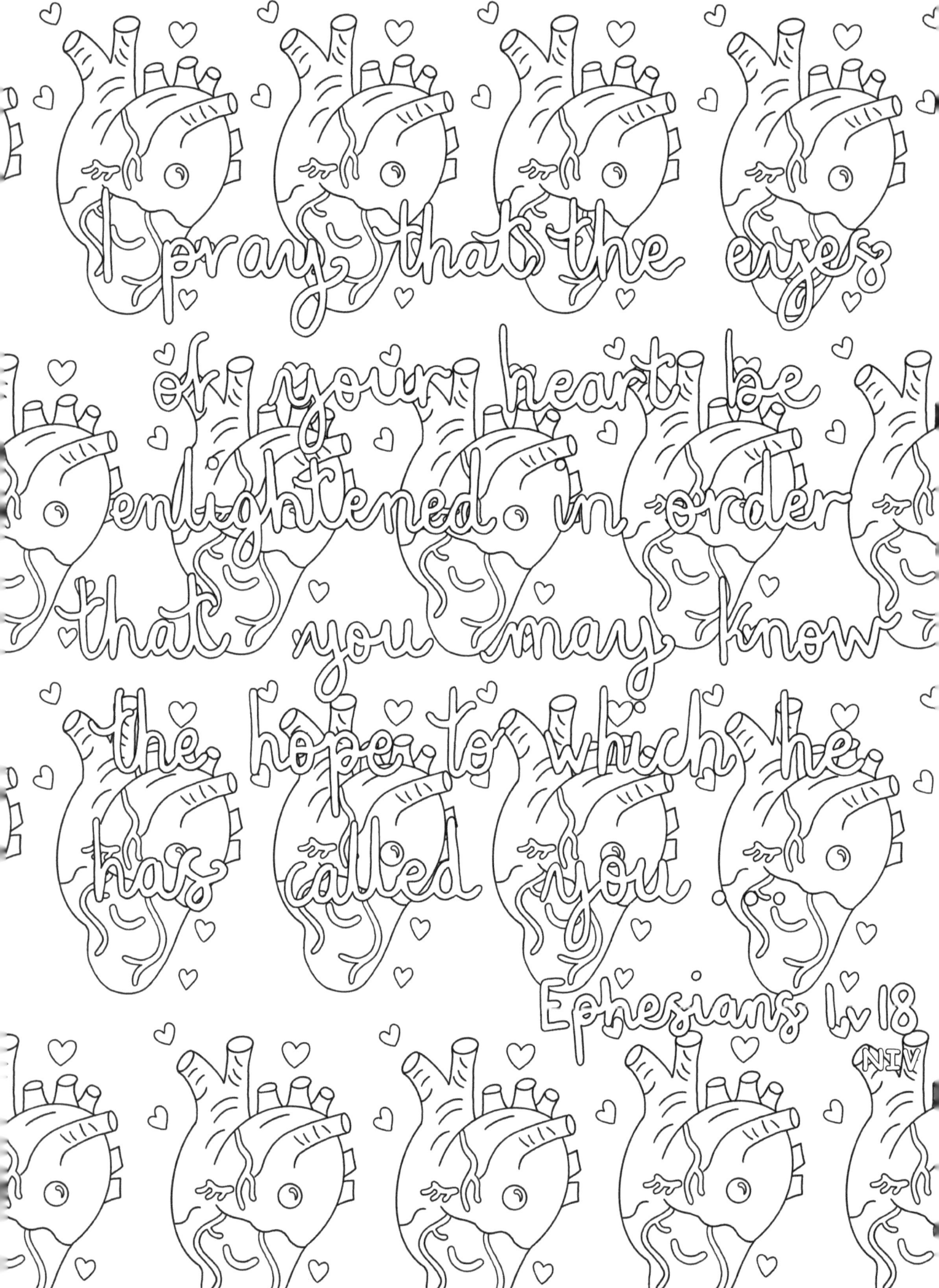

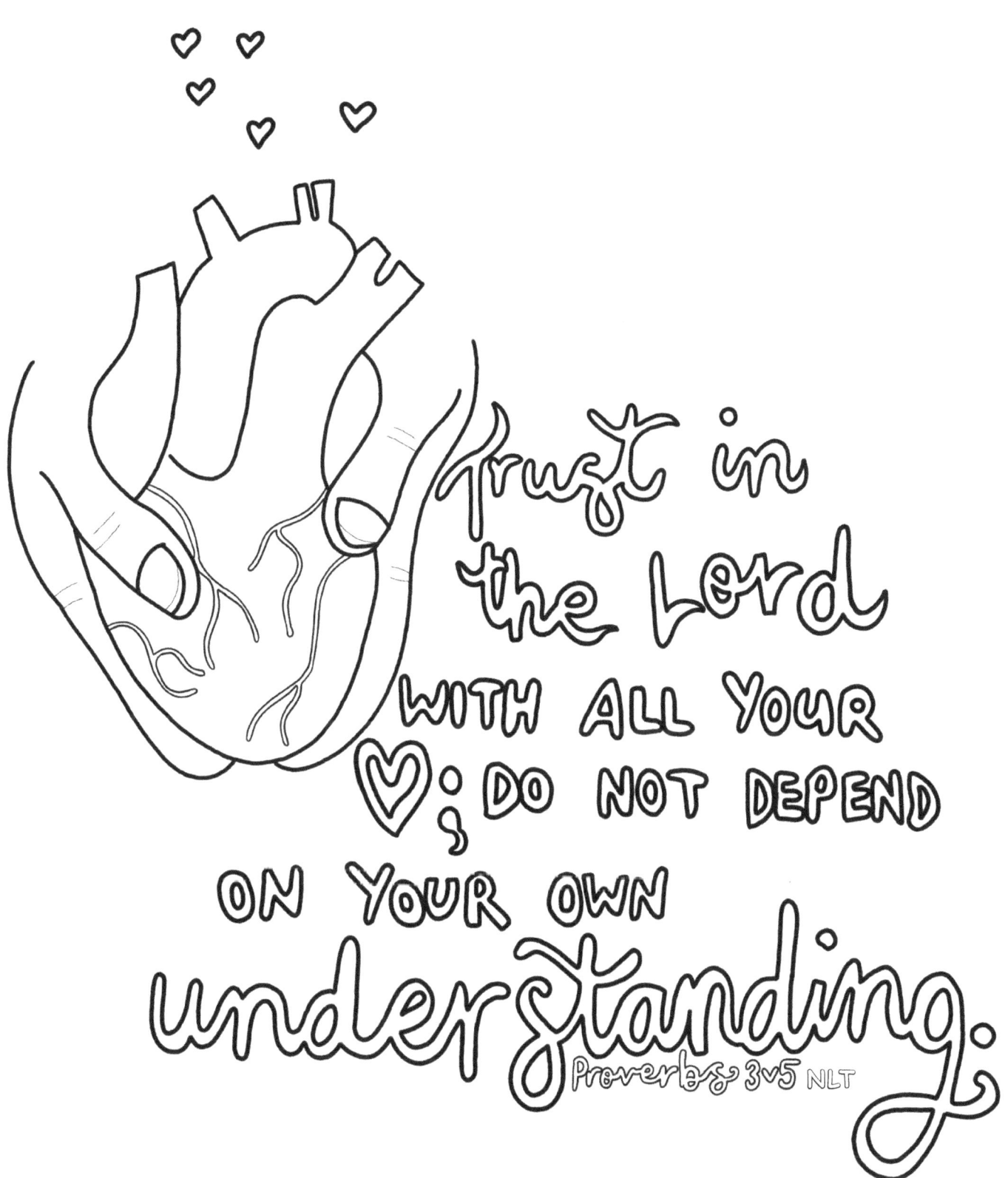

Don't worry about anything; instead, pray about everything. Tell God what you need, and thank Him for all He has done.

Philippians 4v6 NLT

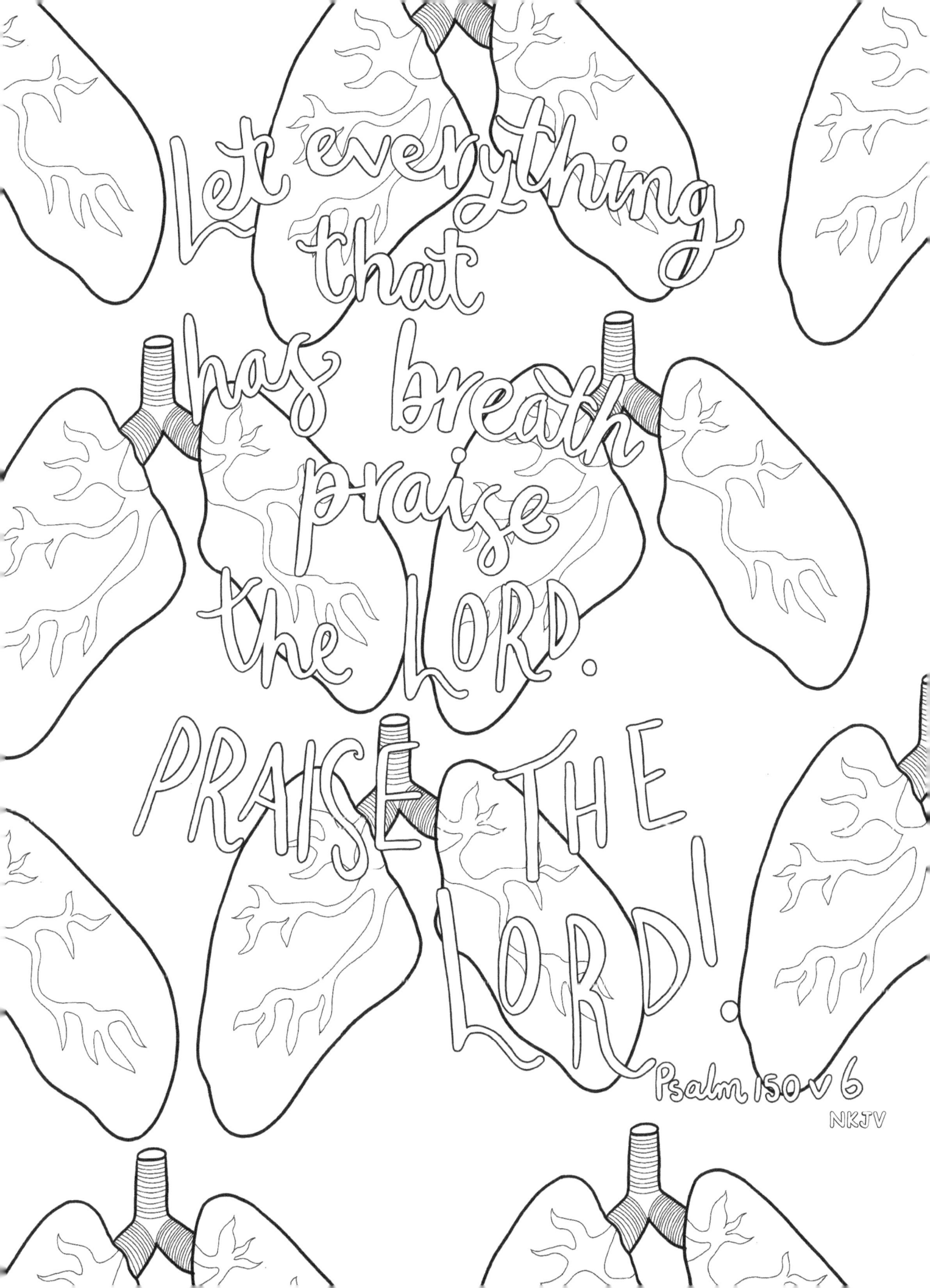

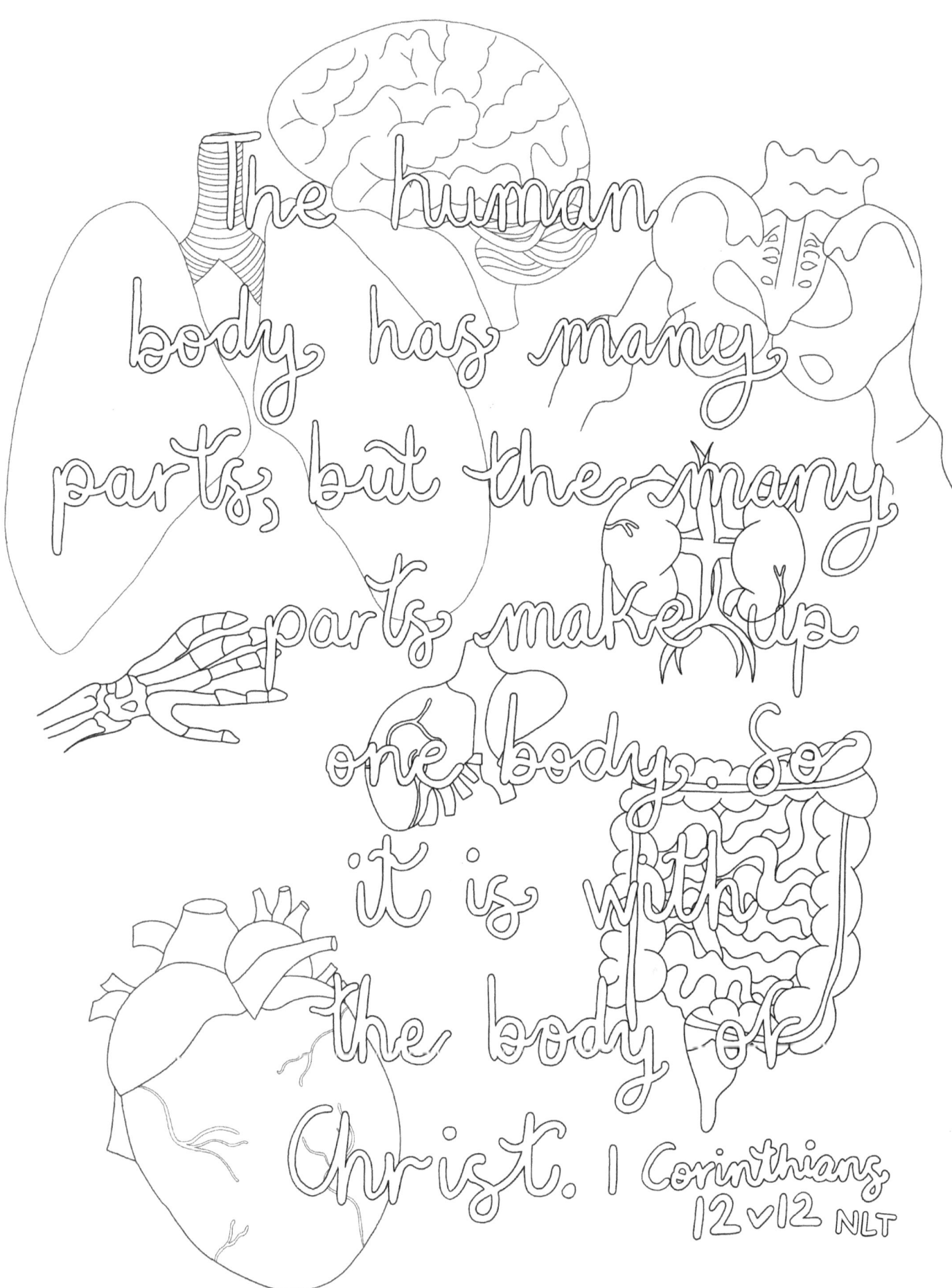

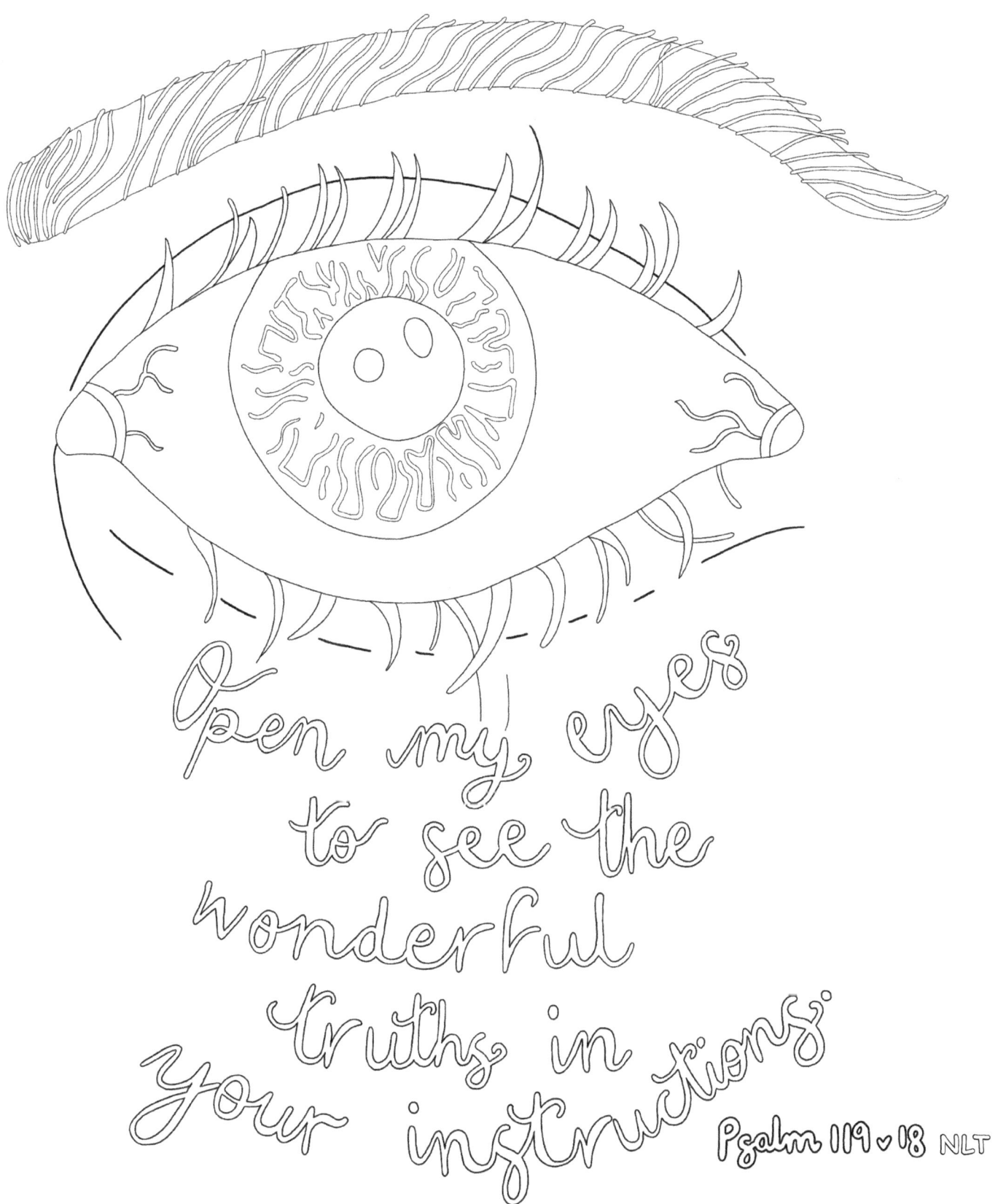

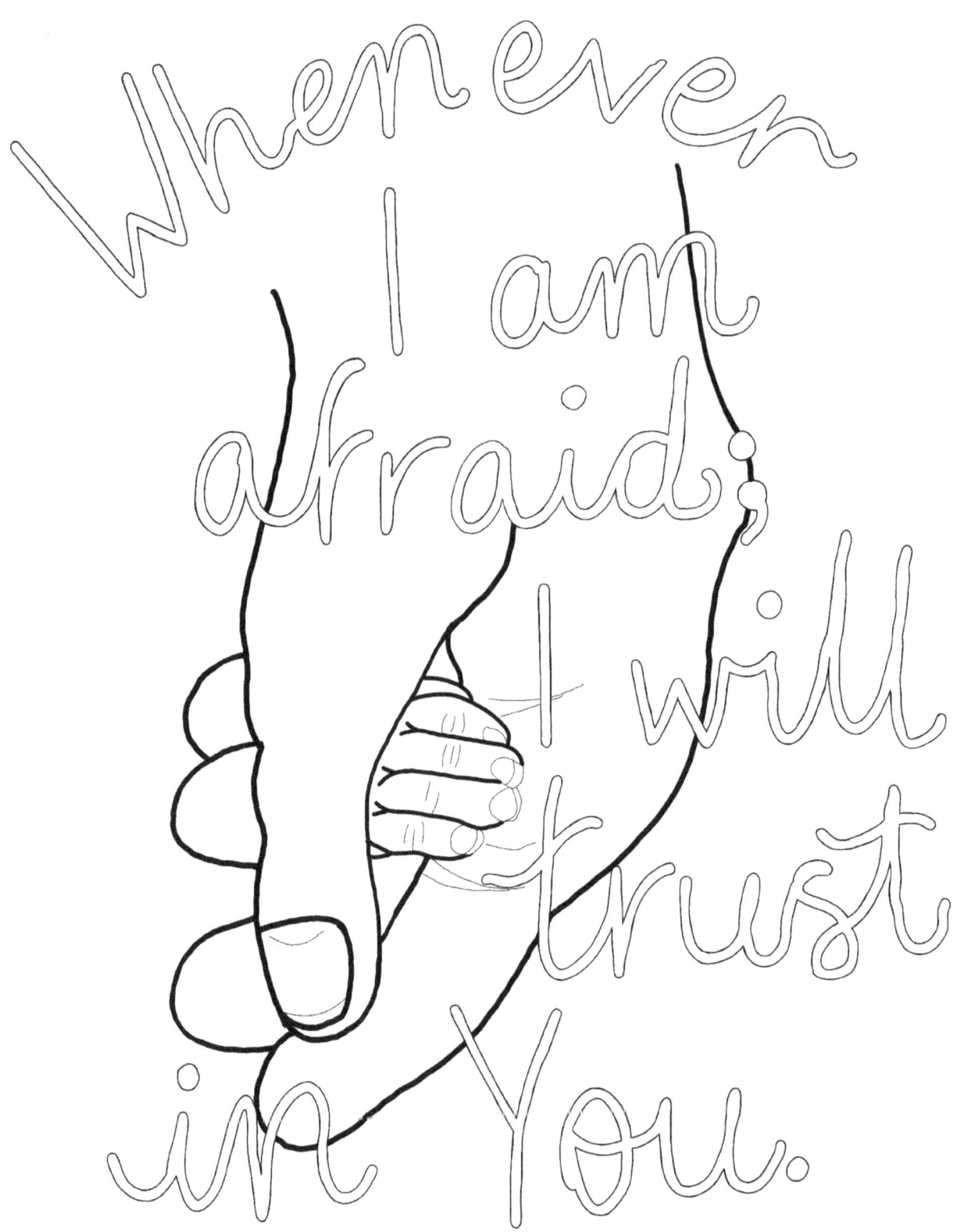

So you have not received a spirit that makes you fearful slaves. Instead, you received God's Spirit when he adopted you as his own children. Now we call him, "Abba Father."

Romans 8v15 NLT

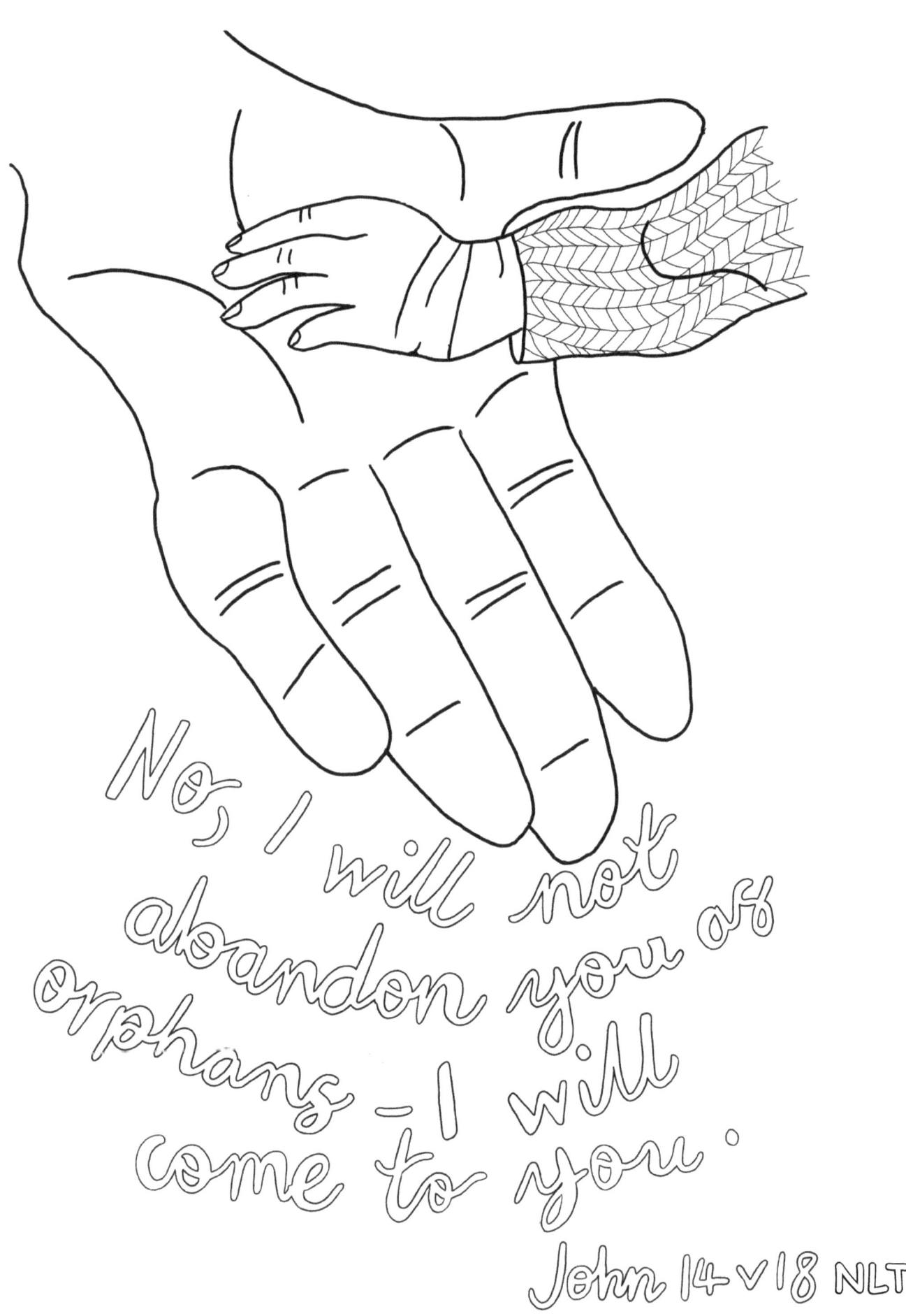

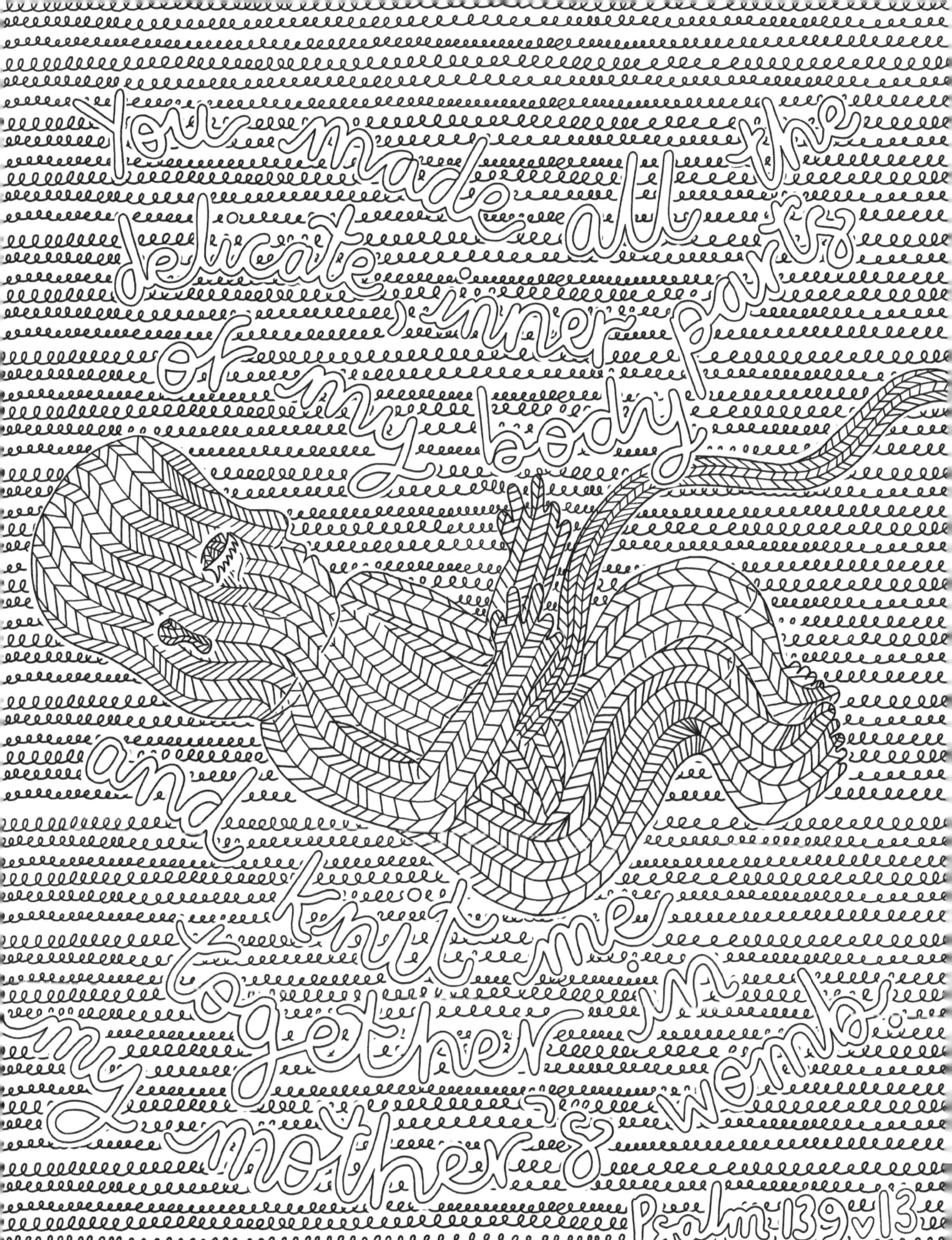

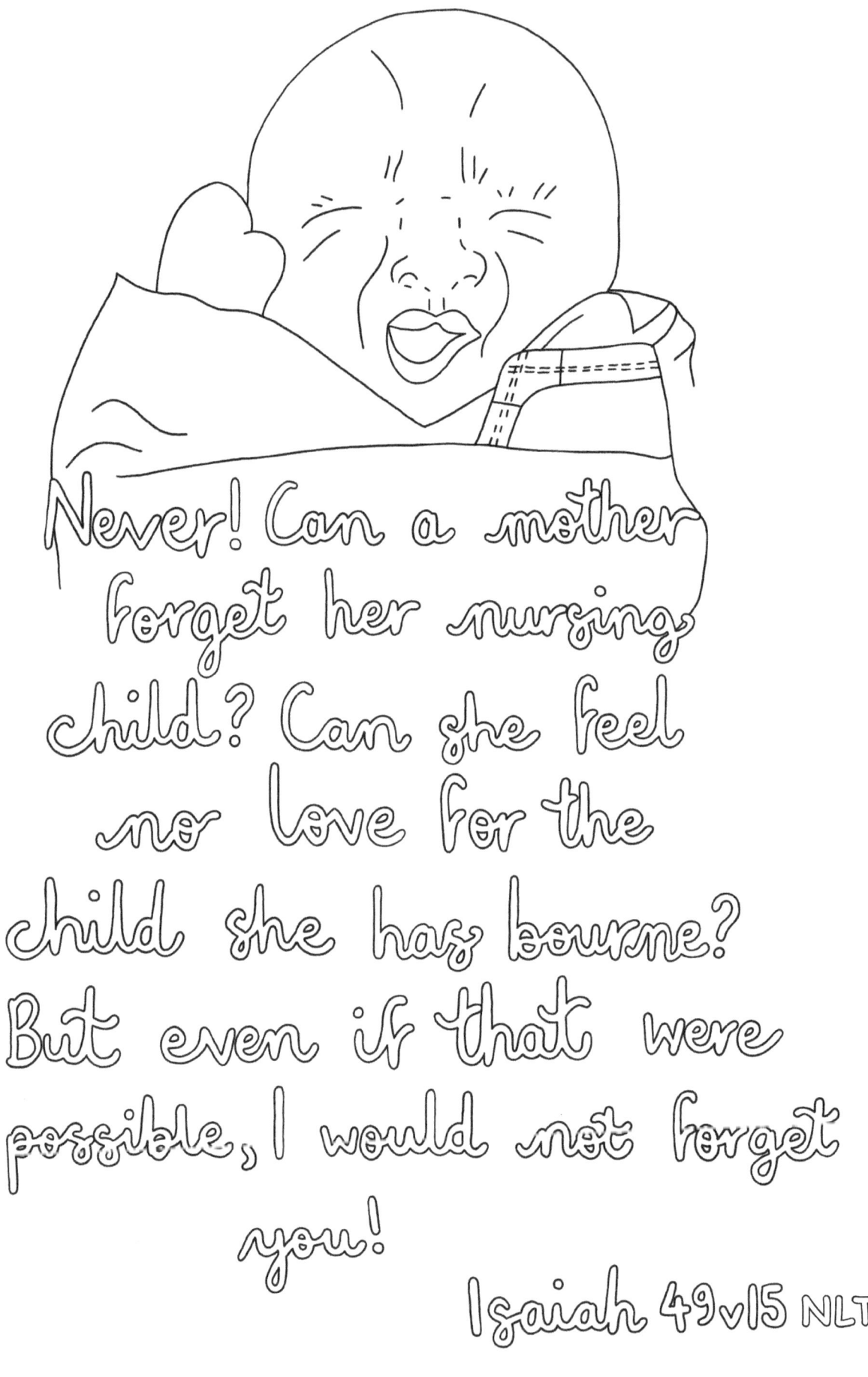

See, I have engraved YOU on the palms of my hands...

Isaiah 49v16 NIV

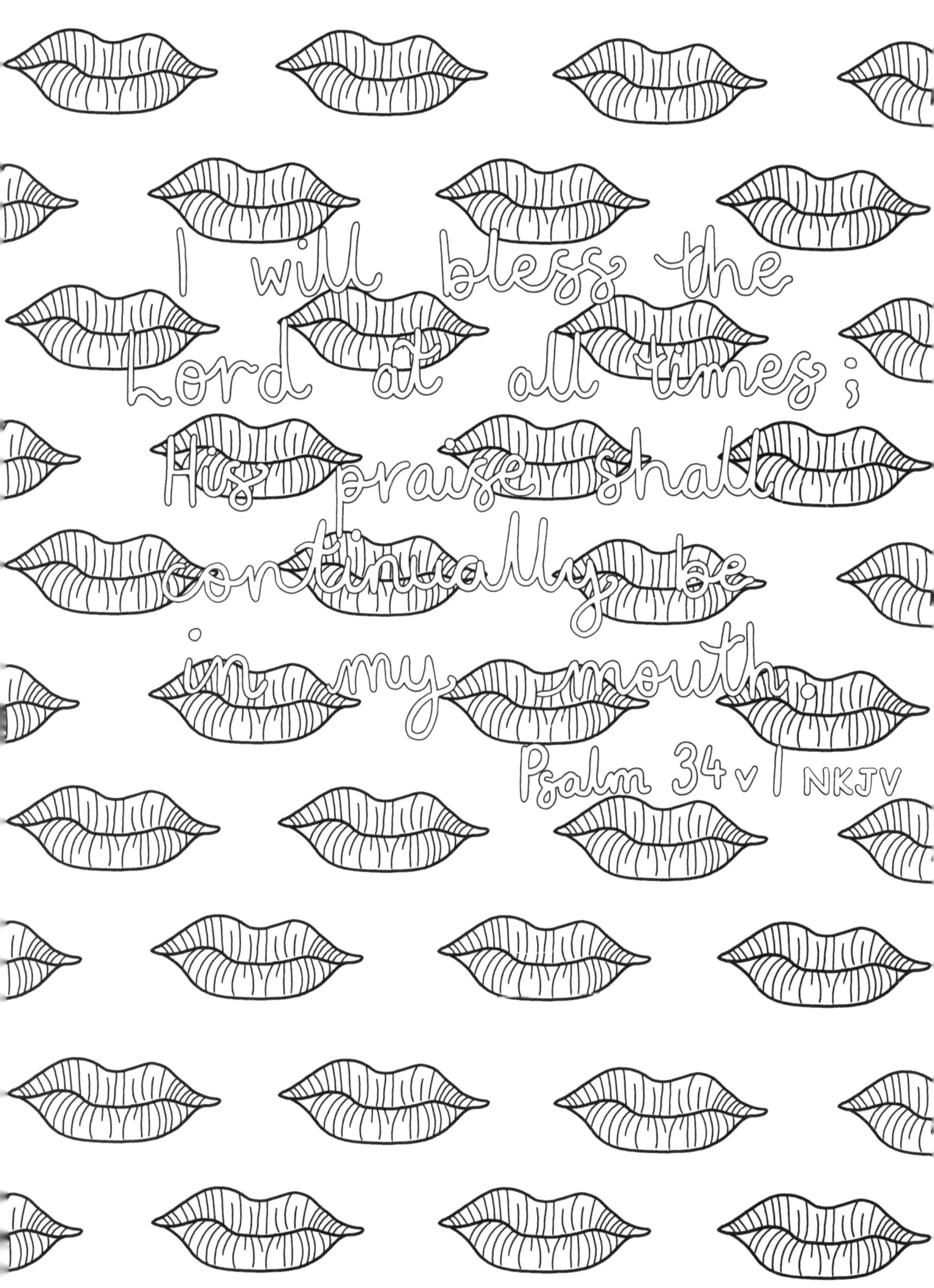

Love each other with genuine affection & take delight in honoring each other.

Romans 12 v 10 NLT

When you go through deep waters, I will be with you. When you go through rivers of difficulty, you will not drown. When you walk through the fire of oppression, you will be burned up; the flames will not consume you.

Isaiah 43v2 NLT

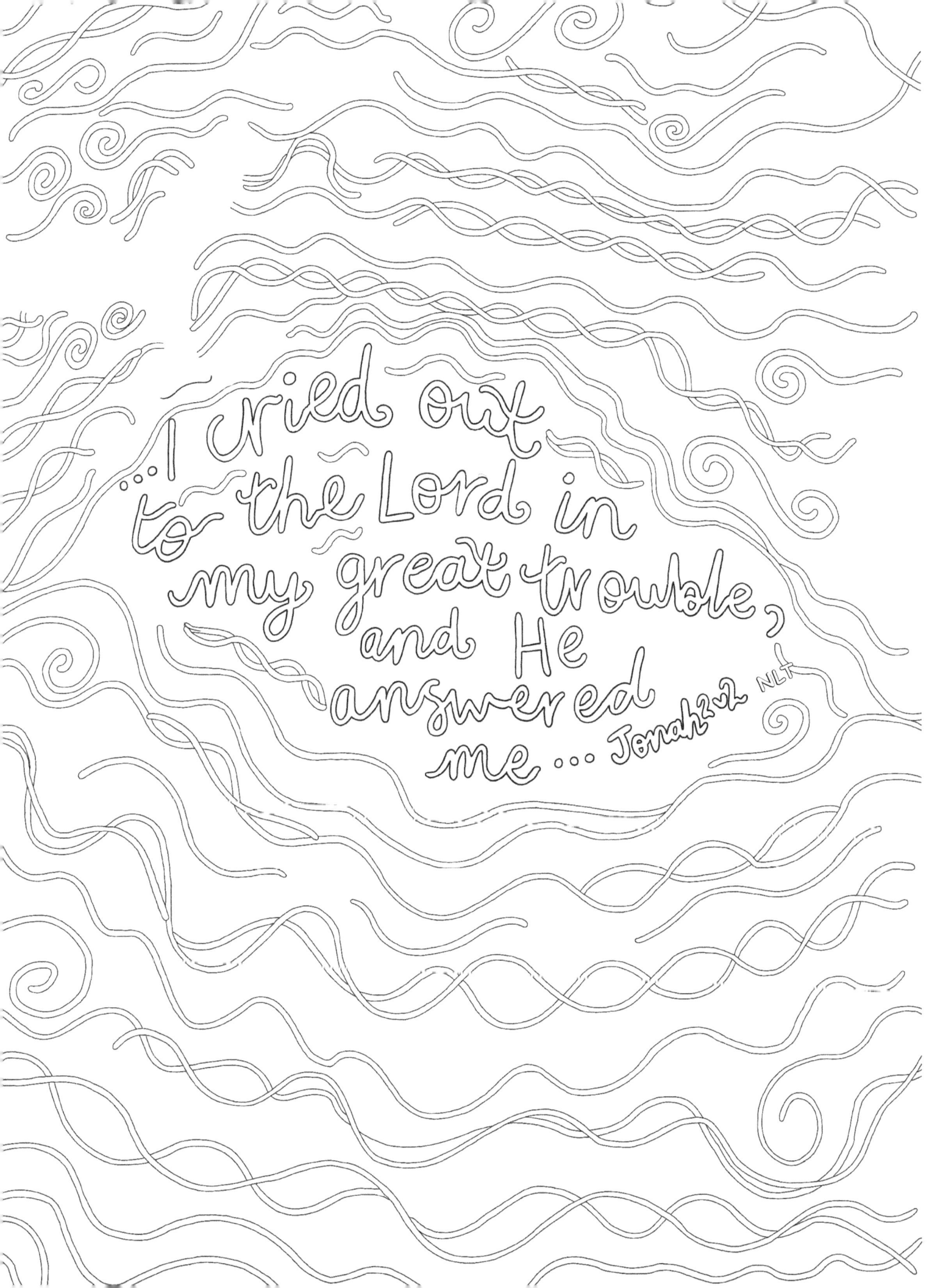

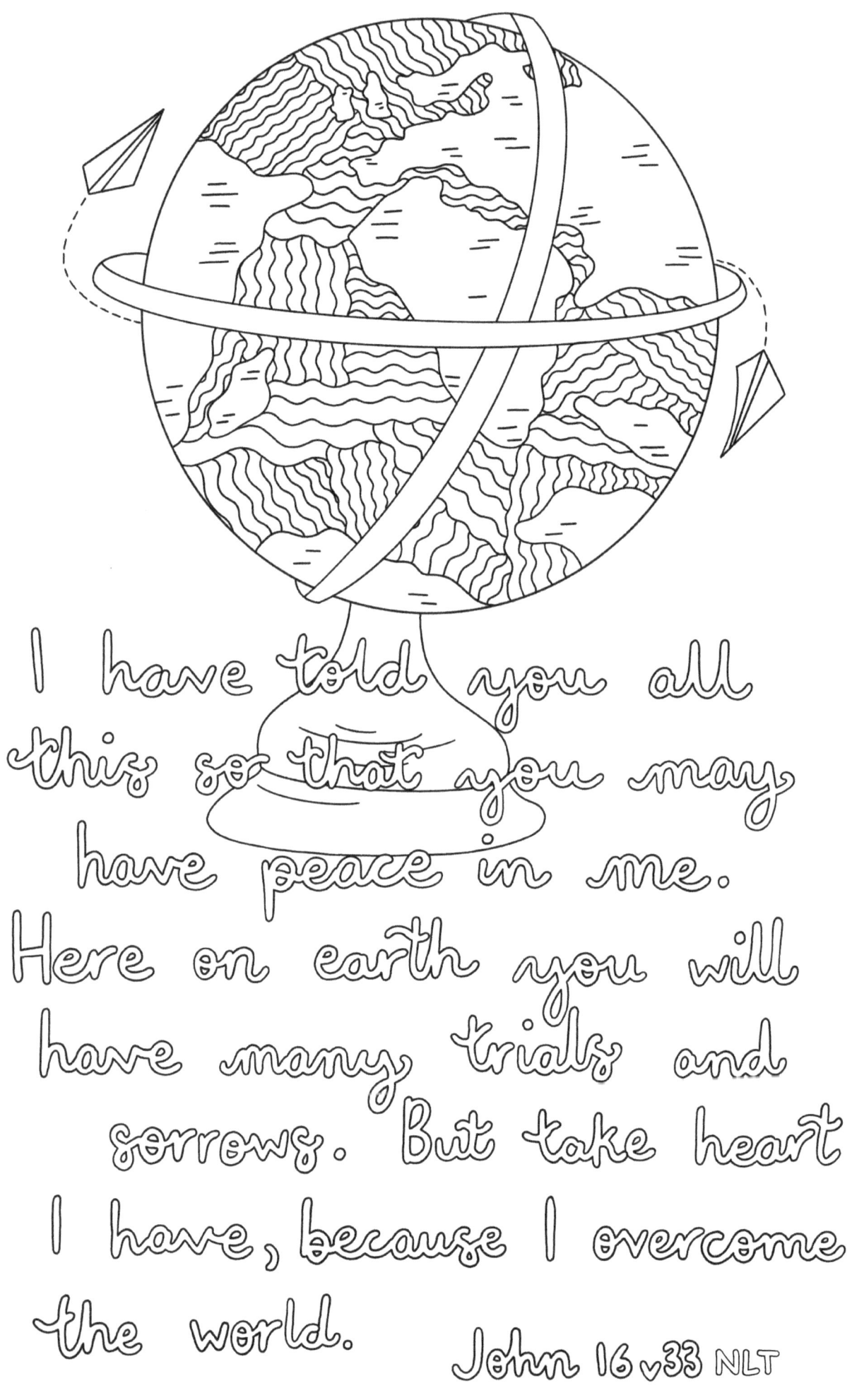

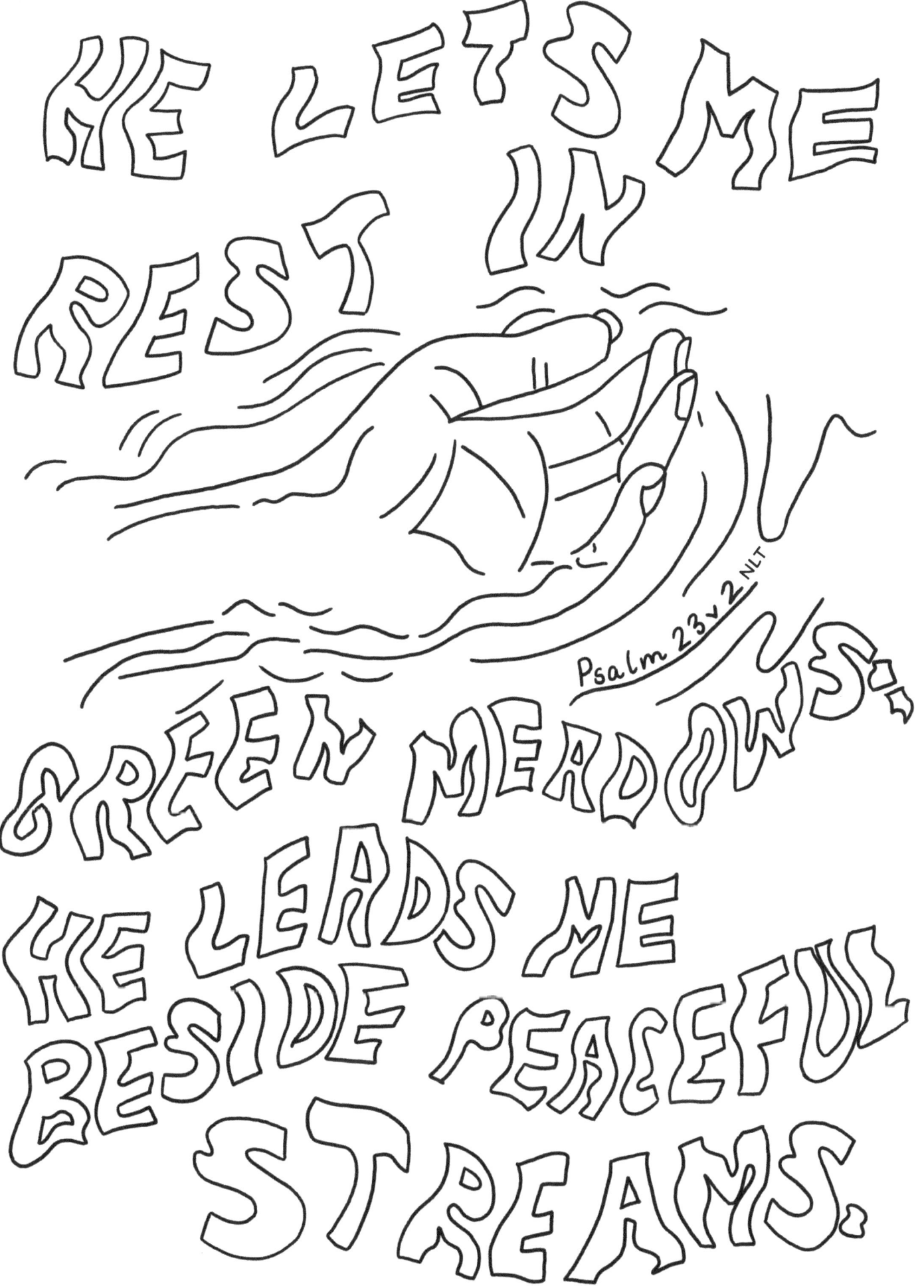

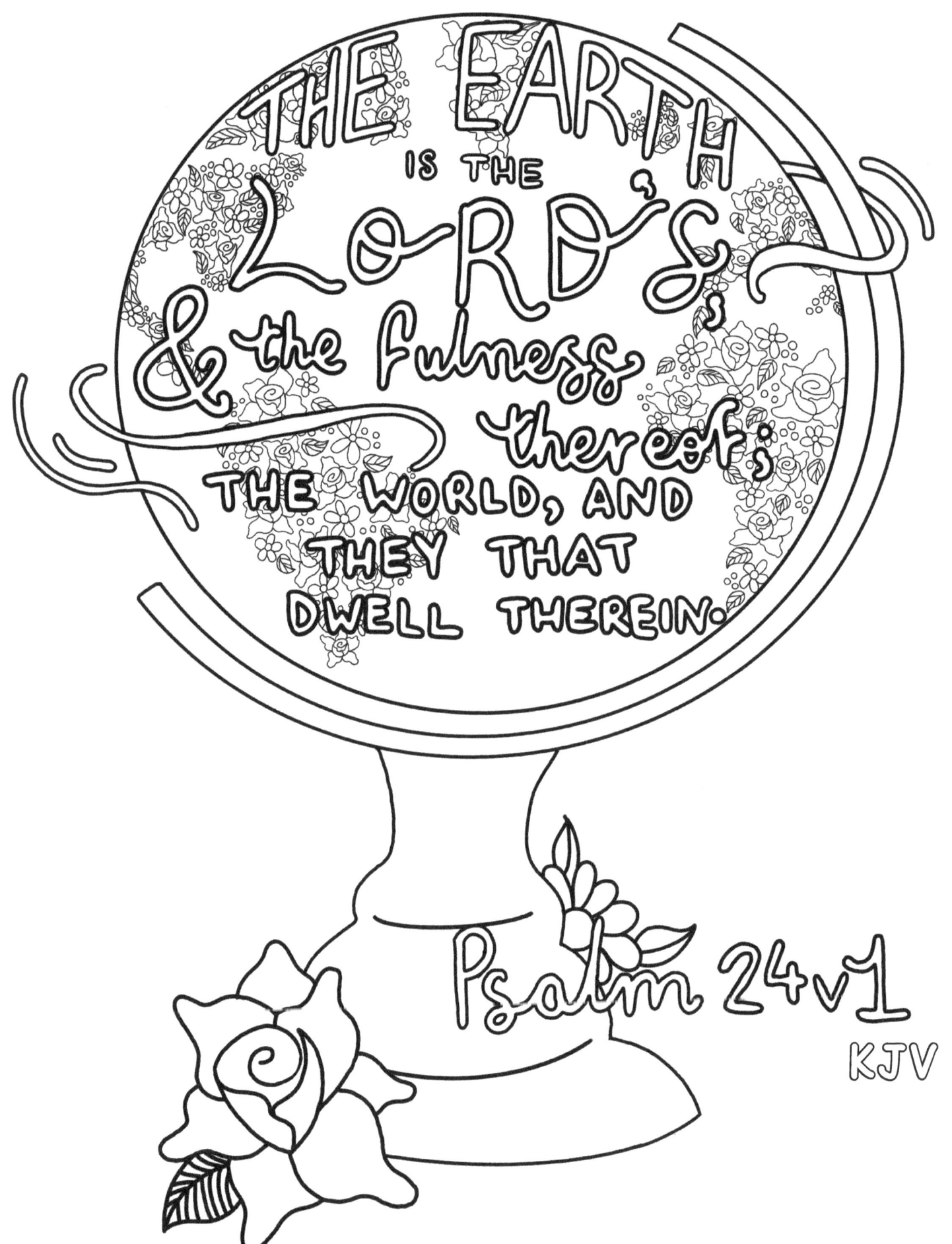

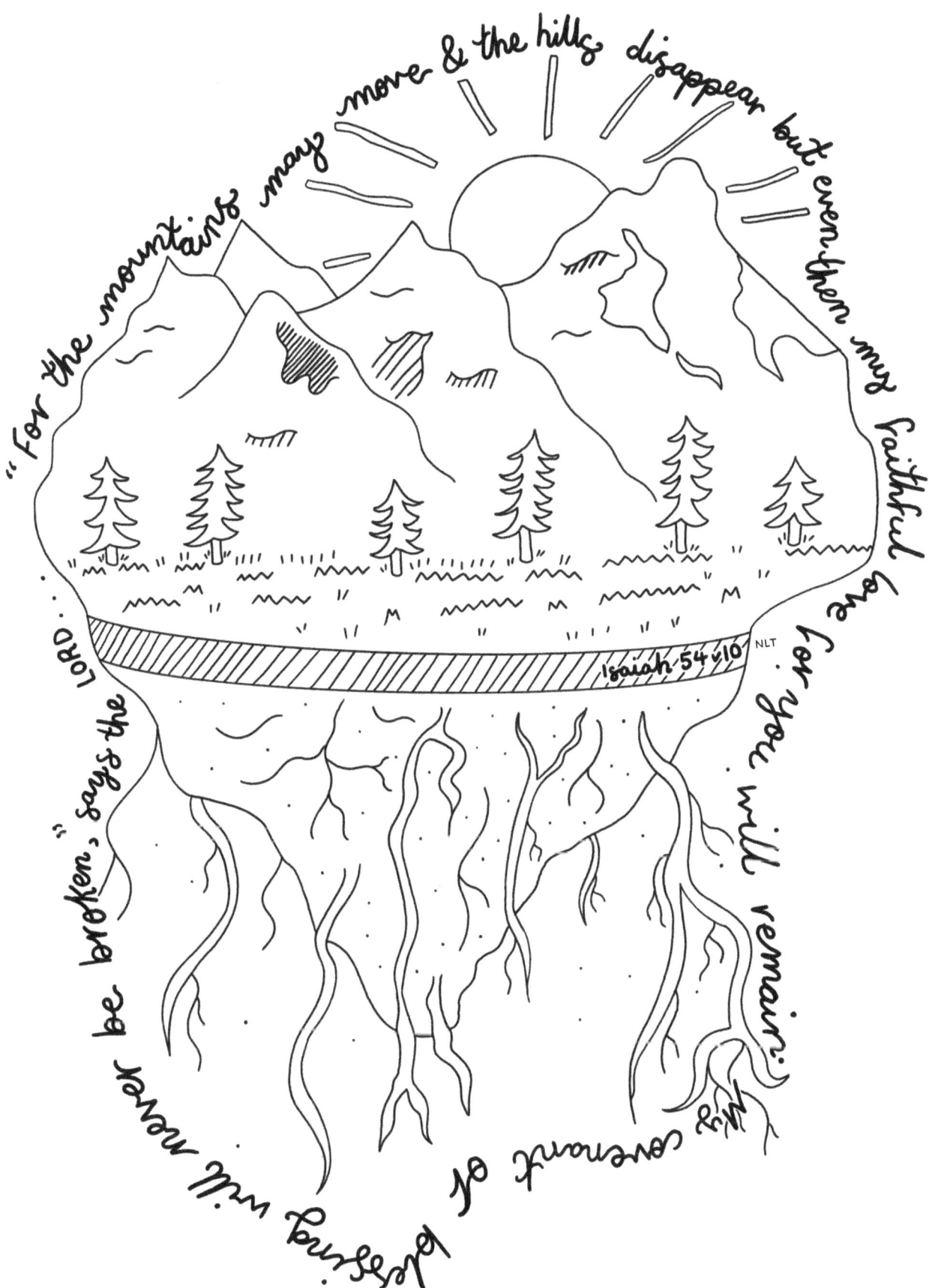

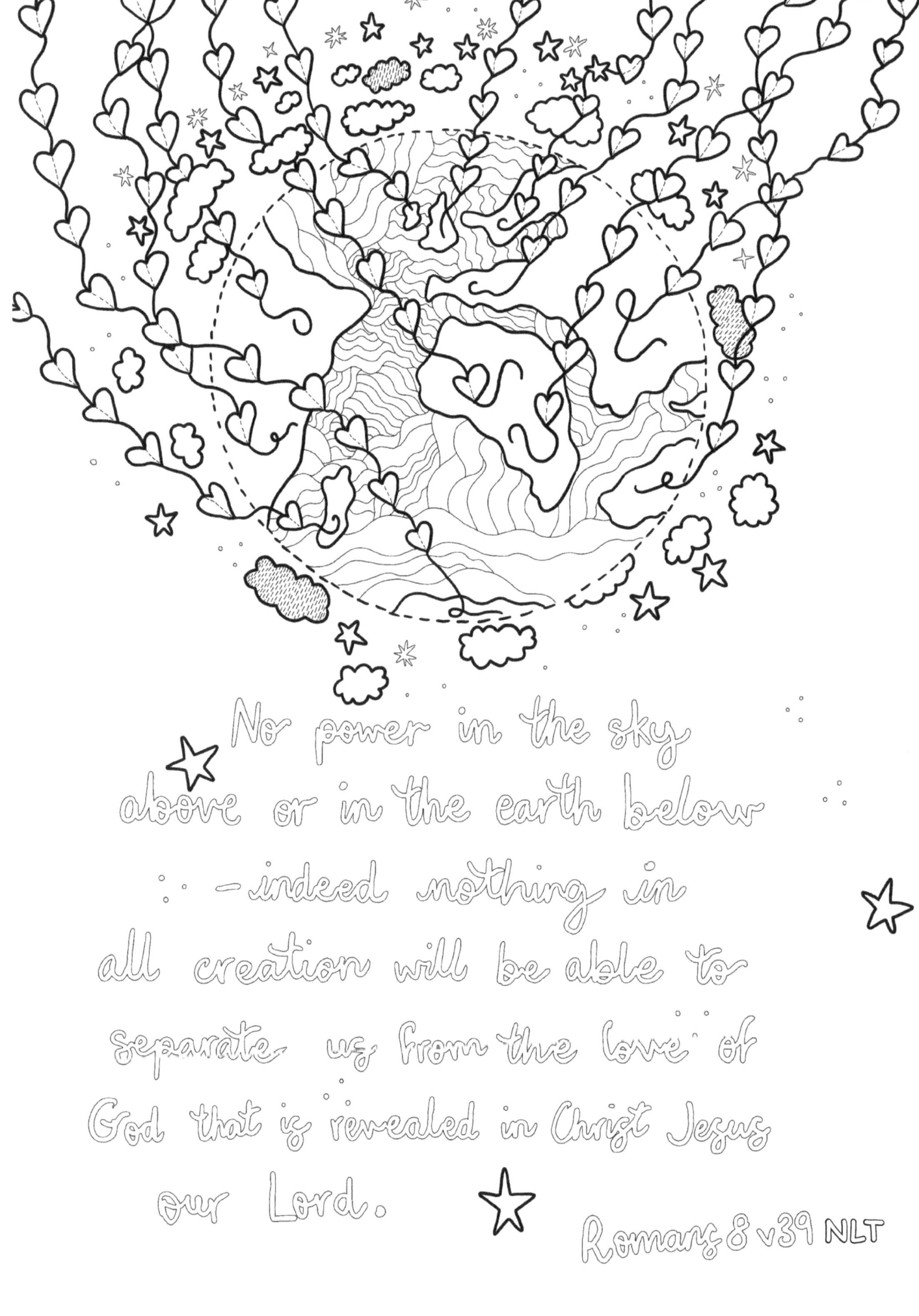

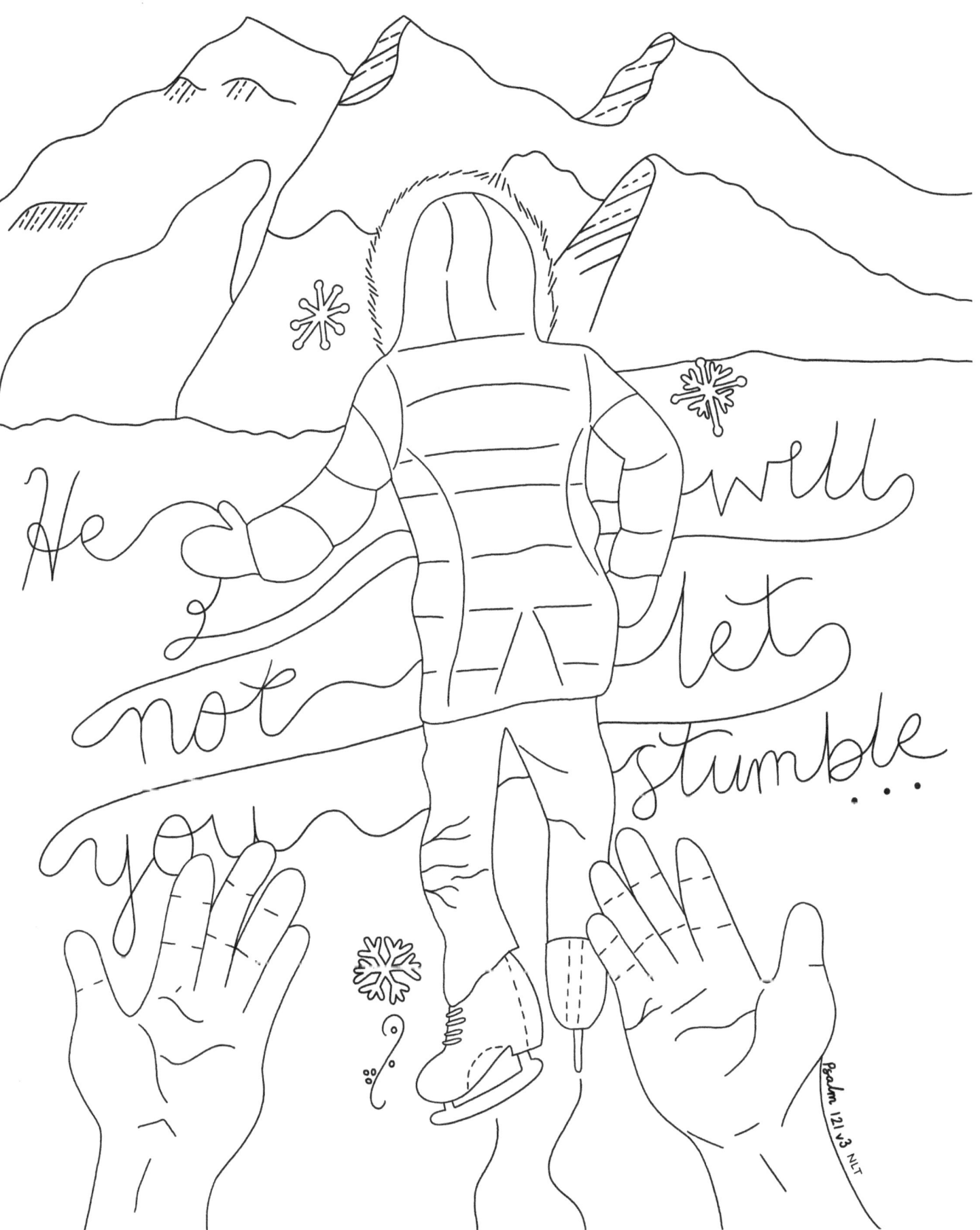

Yet I am confident I will see the LORD's goodness while I am here in the land of the living.

Psalm 27 v 13 NLT

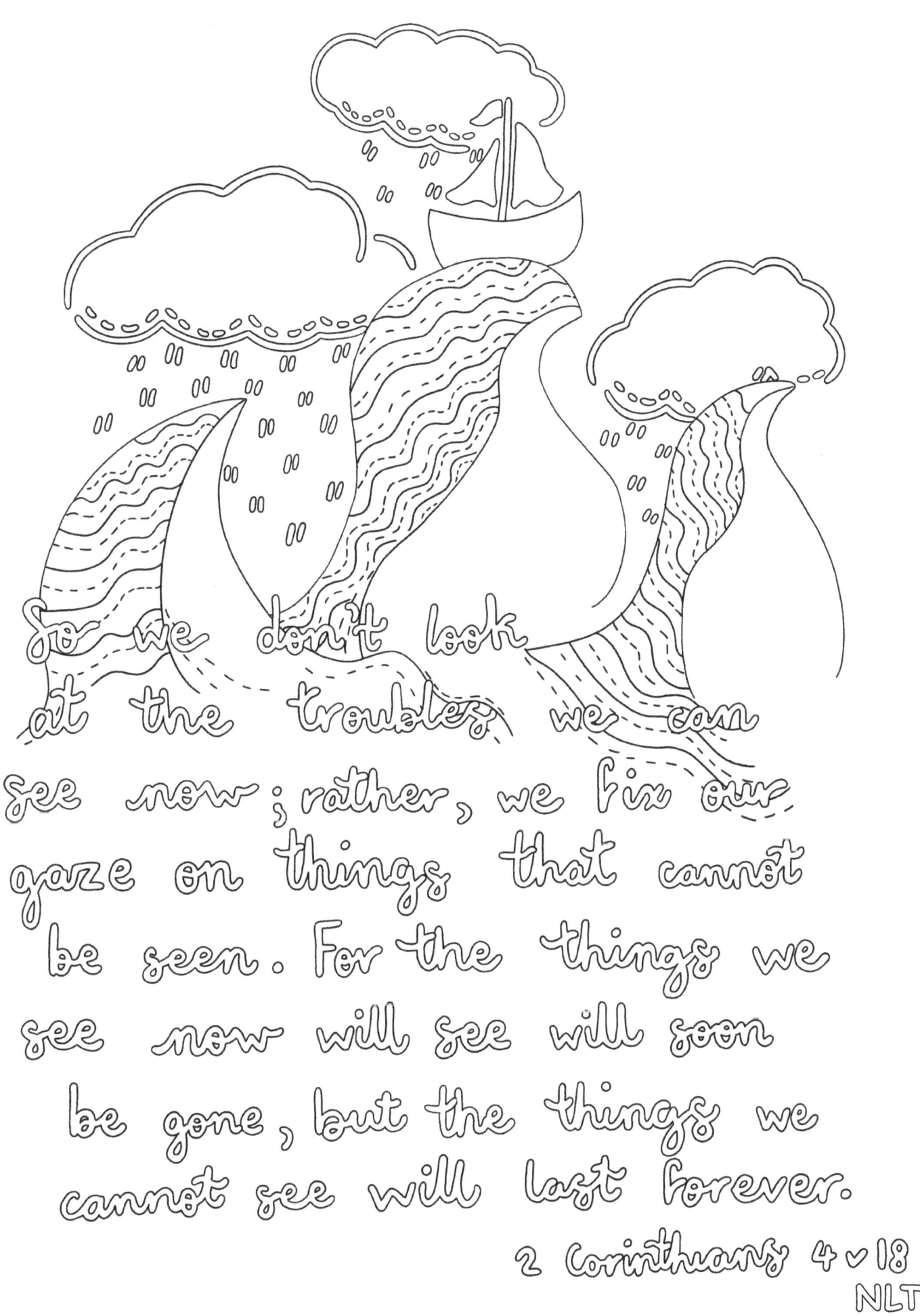

How precious are your thoughts about me, O God. They can't be numbered! I can't even count them. They outnumber the grains of sand! And when I wake up, you are still with me!

Psalm 139 v 17-18
NLT

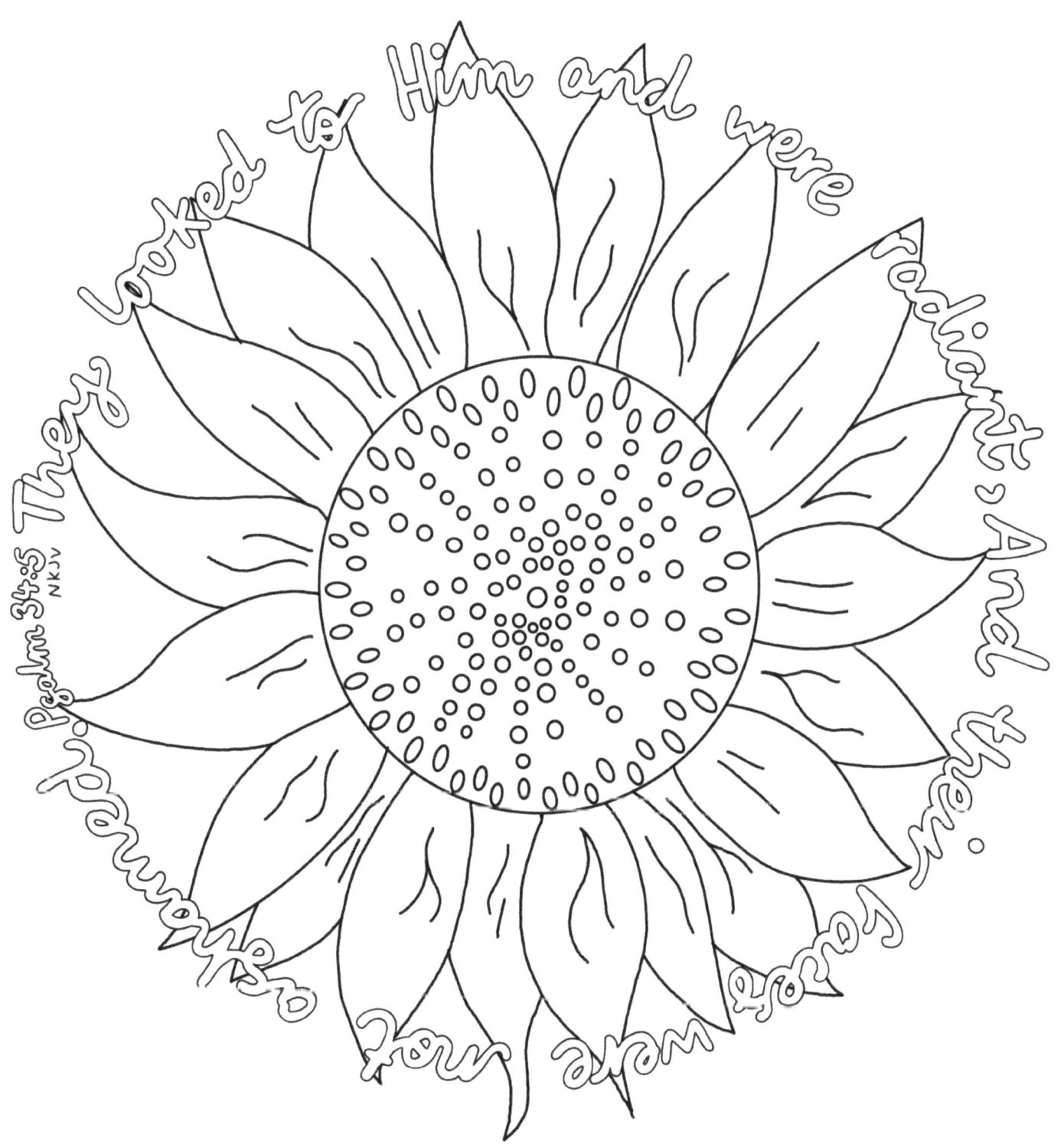

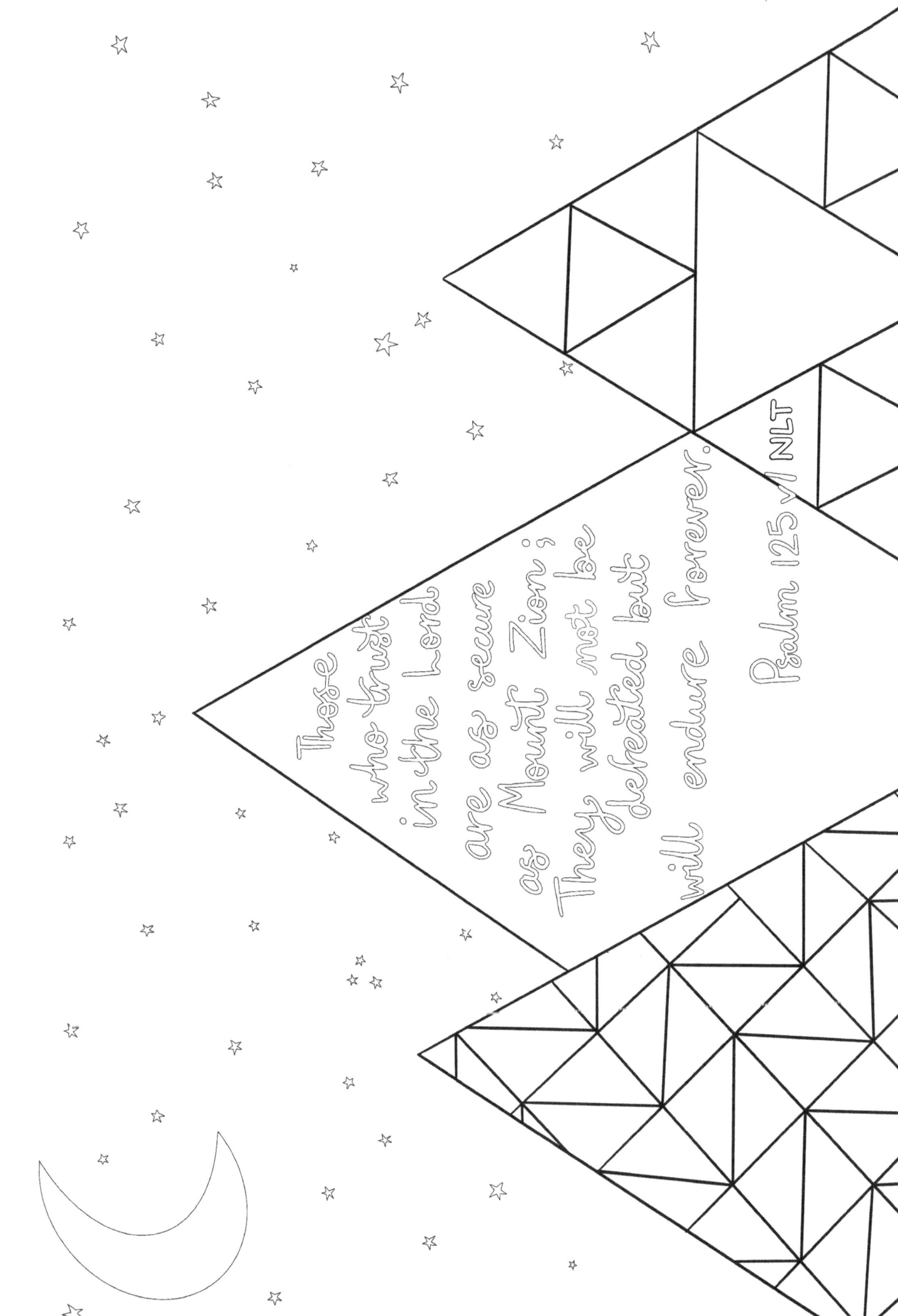

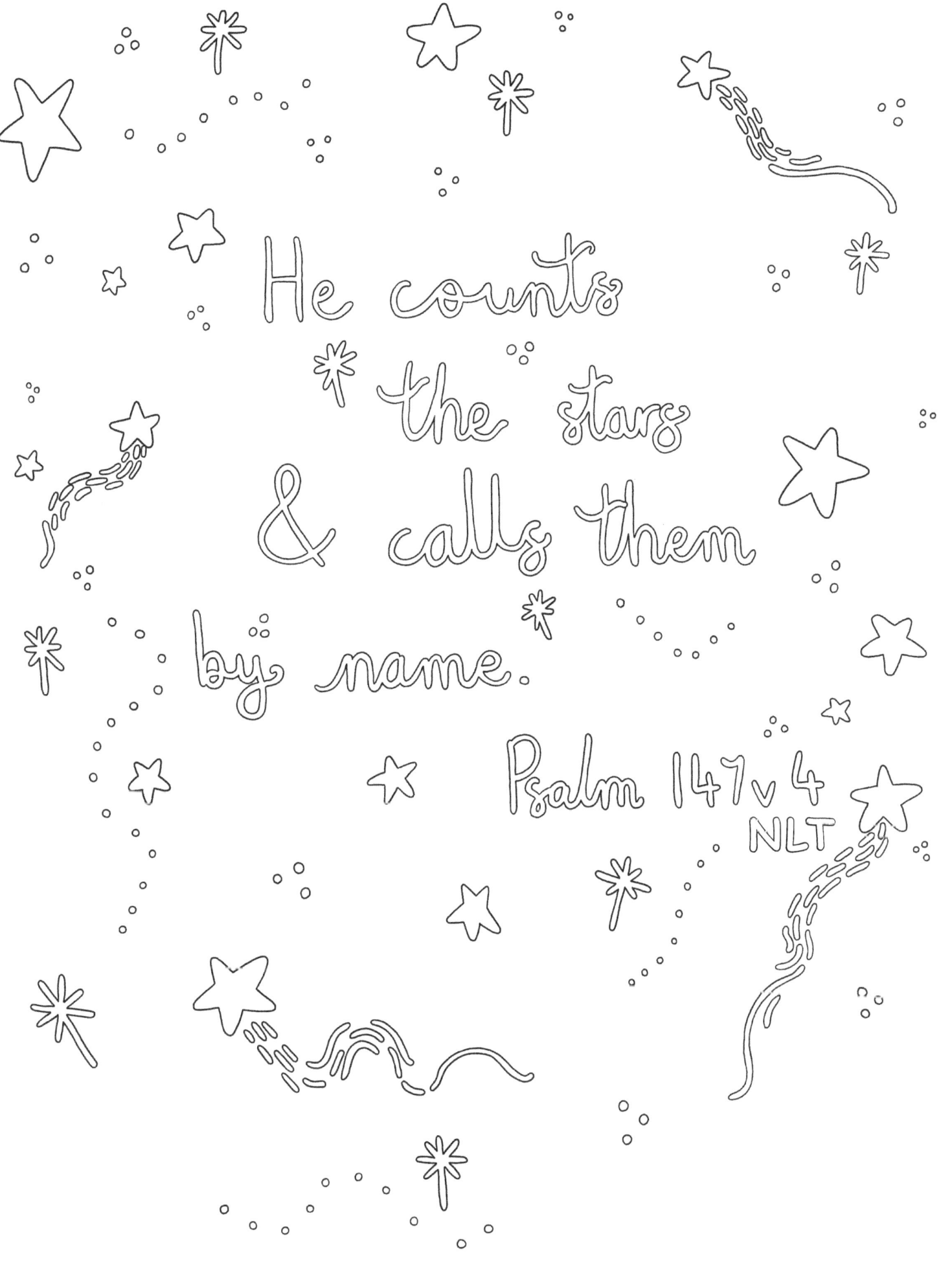